C000263901

Queen Elizabeth's
Book of Oxford

Queen Elizabeth's Book of Oxford

Edited with an Introduction by Louise Durning

Translated by Sarah Knight and Helen Spurling

Bodleian Library
UNIVERSITY OF OXFORD

First published in 2006 by the Bodleian Library
Broad Street, Oxford, OX1 3BG

www.bodleianbookshop.co.uk

ISBN 1 85124 315 1
ISBN 13 978 1 85124 315 0

The English translations were first prepared for publication in Jayne Archer, Elizabeth Clarke, and Elizabeth Goldring (eds.), *Court and Culture in the Reign of Queen Elizabeth I: A New Edition of John Nichols's 'The Progresses of Queen Elizabeth I'*, 4 vols. (OUP, 2007). The publishers are grateful to the editors, the translators and the Delegates of the Oxford University Press for permission to reproduce the texts here.

Designed by Melanie Gradtke
Printed and bound by The University Press, Cambridge
British Library Catalogue in Publishing
A CIP record of this publication is available from the British Library

Cover illustration:
Queen Elizabeth I, artist unknown, *c.* 1575
Robert Dudley, Earl of Leicester, artist unknown, *c.* 1575
National Portrait Gallery, London.

CONTENTS

ACKNOWLEDGEMENTS

Many people have assisted in the preparation of this publication and it is a great pleasure to acknowledge their contributions here.

I am particularly grateful to Martin Kauffmann and Bruce Barker-Benfield, of the Department of Special Collections and Western Manuscripts in the Bodleian Library, for their expert advice on the technical analysis of the manuscript. Special thanks are due to Martin, who encouraged the project to publish the manuscript and who supported it throughout. The staff of Duke Humfrey's library have been unfailingly courteous and helpful. I also thank Michael Riordan, archivist of St John's College, who gave generously of his time and knowledge; Catherine Hilliard, librarian of the college; and Julian Reid, archivist of Corpus Christi College.

I am most grateful to Sarah Knight of the Nichols Project for her many kindnesses and for her generosity in sharing ideas and information. I have also benefited from discussions with Malcolm Airs, Andrew Hegarty, Ian Holgate, Michelle O'Callaghan, Charles Robertson, David Sturdy, Geoffrey Tyack, Malcolm Vale and William Whyte. I am especially indebted to Clare Tilbury who offered many acute observations on the drawings and their context and who kindly read and commented on drafts of the introductory text.

Permission to reproduce images from their collections was kindly given by the National Portrait Gallery, the President and Fellows of St John's College, the President and Fellows of Corpus Christi College and the Warden and Fellows of New College.

Finally, I would like to say a special thank you to Samuel Fanous and Emily Jolliffe of Bodleian Library Publications for their friendly support and encouragement and for the great care they have taken in the development and production of this volume.

Louise Durning
Oxford

LIST OF ILLUSTRATIONS

9. 'Amicitia etiam post mortem durans', from Andrea Alciato, *Emblematum Libellus* (Paris, 1534).
Bodleian Library, Douce A. 438.

INTRODUCTION

Louise Durning

> Behold, (most distinguished Princess Elizabeth) you hold a topographical delineation of the Colleges and public Schools of your University of Oxford, partly represented by the draughtsman's pen, partly in poetic verse ... so that you might have the University's entire likeness to hand, as if laid out before your eyes....

On 31 August 1566 Queen Elizabeth began the first visit of her reign to the University of Oxford. As she made her triumphal entry through the city she was presented with the sight of the whole university laid out before her eyes. The streets were lined on both sides with all the scholars of Oxford, drawn up in order of their degrees and clothed in their distinctive dress, kneeling and cheering 'vivat regina' as she passed. First came the undergraduates, followed by the Bachelors, then the Masters, and finally, as she reached the gates of Christ Church, where she would stay for the next six days, all the Doctors of Theology, Medicine and Law.[1] This marshalling of the scholars must have presented a striking image of the university as a corporate body, a coherent and ordered community of loyal subjects. But, in one of the many gifts presented to her during the course of the visit, she was presented with a different representation of the university, embodied in the small manuscript book reproduced here.[2] In the drawings it contains of the colleges and schools of Oxford we have, for the first time, a representation of the university as its buildings.

The manuscript presents an imaginary journey around these buildings, conducted in the form of a Latin verse dialogue between the Queen and Robert Dudley, Earl of Leicester, the recently appointed Chancellor of the university and, as such, the Queen's official host for the visit.[3] It was the work of two Oxford scholars: Thomas Neale, Regius Professor of Hebrew, who composed the Latin (and Hebrew) text, and John Bereblock, Fellow of Exeter College, who made the drawings.[4]

Neale's presentation to the Queen of their little book is recorded in a number of contemporary accounts of the Royal Visit, one of which even describes the Queen accepting it with great pleasure, 'as if she had never before received a greater or better gift' (although, as this may have been written by Bereblock himself, some exaggeration may be suspected).[5] The manuscript did not stay in royal hands, however, and entered the Bodleian Library in 1630 as a gift from one John More.[6] The identity of this donor, and thus some clue as to the possible route through which he could have acquired it, cannot be established with certainty and this enigmatic provenance has led some to question whether this is indeed the Queen's own copy.[7] Yet the exquisite care taken in the production of the manuscript, with its fine italic script, its carefully controlled page design and its richly detailed drawings, declares its character as a high-status presentation copy.[8] It is, moreover, written in the same hand, and carries a version of the same illustrated frontispiece, as a second manuscript given to the Queen by Neale on the same occasion, and which is still held in the Royal Collection in the British Library.[9] On the basis of this evidence there seems little reason to doubt that this is indeed 'the very book which was put into Queen Elizabeth's hands.'[10]

The Queen's Book has often been described as a 'guidebook', but the 'Topographical Delineation', as Neale titled it, is much more complex than such a description would suggest and it will be the purpose of this introduction to analyse the design and purpose of the manuscript in order to gain a better understanding of its importance.

Perhaps the most significant aspect of the book is the series of drawings it contains, which are not only of local significance, as the earliest known images of the colleges and schools of Oxford, but of national significance. They belong to the earliest period of the development of topographical representation in England and mark one of the first attempts by an English draughtsman to create a systematic visual record of a specific place.[11] In order to understand why these drawings were made, and why they take the particular form they do, they need to be considered in relation to the particular circumstances of the Royal Visit as well as to the more general context of a growing interest in topography. No less important is the question of their relationship to the literary framework within which they are set. Indeed, the particular combination of word and image developed by Neale and Bereblock for their 'description' of Oxford deserves to be seen as itself a novel creation, which draws upon and reinvents some of the newest fashions in the literary and visual culture of the English renaissance.

'THESE FIRST ATTEMPTS AT A NEW UNDERTAKING'

During the six days of the Queen's stay in Oxford, the university sought to show itself off to best advantage and to make the necessary demonstrations of gratitude and support for the new Elizabethan order. The triumphal entry into the city, punctuated with speeches of welcome in Latin and Greek, was followed by a programme of formal academic disputations in St Mary's Church, with performance of plays in the evenings in the hall of Christ Church, transformed into a 'roman palace' for the occasion.[12] The programme of events closely followed that developed for the Queen's visit to Cambridge University, undertaken two years earlier, and, as at Cambridge, the visit was also the occasion for the production of large quantities of orations and verse in praise of the Queen.[13] Some of these were delivered orally, some presented in manuscript form, and many more were pasted up on the walls and doors of the colleges. The Latin and Greek of these orations and verses not only demonstrated the learning of their authors; they also complimented the Queen herself, famed as the Learned Queen, who spoke Latin and Greek and was skilled in the same patterns of rhetoric and classical learning as the scholars of both universities.[14]

It is not difficult to imagine the atmosphere of competitive rhetorical invention which would have informed the scholars' public displays of literary skill and in which Neale and Bereblock devised their new genre of 'topographical delineation'.[15] In the dedicatory preface to the dialogue, Neale makes explicit claims for its novelty, asking the Queen to show favour to 'these first attempts at a new undertaking' *(dabis tamen (ut spero) veniam primis hisce conatibus in re nova)* (fol. iv). Setting aside the conventional combination of humility and calculated self-advertisement which was the standard currency of dedicatory prefaces of the period, their Topographical Delineation could indeed claim to be a 'new thing'. The combination of image and verse sets it apart from the many other demonstrations of literary invention produced for the visit, and, by implication, raises graphic skill to the same level of scholarly prestige as literary composition. Although Neale appears to make an apology for the drawings, suggesting that they are the work of a 'duller' *(crassiore)* pen, made worthy of the Queen's sight only through their placing within a framework of verse, this is a conventionalized expression of modesty (fol. 4). The fulsome praise of the 'marvellous' *(mira)* drawings put into Leicester's mouth later in the text may give a clearer indication of how he hoped they would be received (fol. 13ᵛ). In the approved humanist manner, he justifies the experiment by reference to a classical authority, with a quote from Horace's *Art of Poetry* that 'for painters and poets there should always be an equal power of venturing whatever they like' *(pictoribus atque poetis quidlibet audendi semper fuit aequa potestas)*.

Of course, as Alistair Fowler has noted, 'new literary genres seldom (perhaps never) appear out of the blue. Instead they combine or adapt the formal repertoires of existing genres.'[16] In the discussion that follows I will examine a range of contemporary genres that may prove suggestive for understanding the relation between image and text in this manuscript, but first it will be necessary to look in more detail at each of these components: the dialogue and the pictures.

THE DIALOGUE

Neale's choice of the dialogue form as the rhetorical model for the text was in itself unusual. Although well established in contemporary humanist writing as a mode for the analysis of intellectual or moral concepts, notably in Sir Thomas More's *Utopia*, it was not a conventional form for occasional verse.[17] As a 'real person' dialogue, in which the author puts words into the mouths of such powerful figures as Leicester and the Queen, it could also be considered a potentially risky choice, but this device could also allow the verses to be received as a gesture of deferential modesty, investing the authority of the text in the noble speakers rather than the author himself.[18] More specifically, it may have been intended to evoke the type of dialogue associated with Italian court culture, exemplified by Baldassare Castiglione's *Il Cortegiano (The Courtier)*, in which elevated protagonists discourse on some moral or intellectual topic in elegant and graceful conversation.[19] The informal tone of Leicester's exchanges with the Queen establishes a sociable, even intimate style, creating the fiction of an extempore conversation, marked by spontaneity and word play. An important sub-theme of Neale's dialogue, the praise of Leicester, is played out through a running pun on *dux* (leader/general/Duke) and *comes* (companion/Earl), establishing and celebrating Leicester's role as the noble companion and guide to the Queen.[20] This was perhaps the most attractive feature of the dialogue for Neale's purposes: the opportunity it provided to pay a double compliment, not only to the Queen but also to Leicester, the university's new Chancellor and a powerful figure in the internal politics of the university. It is thus Leicester, not Neale, who takes the Queen on this 'virtual progress' around his own little realm, and who speaks as the champion of learning.

The conceit of the imaginary itinerary structures the whole composition. The action opens at Woodstock, the Royal Palace near Oxford, where Leicester and the Queen are preparing to leave on horseback for the city, and as they ride towards Oxford he describes to the Queen the famous buildings she will see. As the dialogue unfolds, the Chancellor considers each college or school in turn, commenting on its worthy founder and epitomizing some aspect of its fame. At regular intervals the Queen interjects or asks questions in return and the dialogue ends as they arrive at Christ Church, where Thomas Neale himself is introduced, waiting to present his gift to the Queen, and to deliver the Hebrew verse and oration with which the manuscript concludes.

But what kind of itinerary is this and what kind of topography of Oxford does it represent? Can it even be mapped on to the streets of Oxford? The frequent use of locational phrases in the dialogue, as the discussion moves from one place to the next, ('on the western side ...'; 'now having ventured outside the walls of the city ...') reinforces the topographical theme and the verses accompanying the images of All Souls, Merton, Corpus and Oriel colleges indicate sequence with even greater show of precision, indicating that they are, respectively, the fourth, fifth, sixth and seventh colleges to be encountered on the imaginary journey. Unfortunately, the manuscript was reassembled out of order during its rebinding in the seventeenth century and these colleges now appear in the wrong sequence, but it is possible to reconstruct the probable original sequence by comparison with a contemporary copy of Neale's text which does exhibit the order suggested by the verses.[21] From this, a clearer picture emerges of the topographical logic governing the composition and it becomes obvious that it is one in which mere physical proximity has been subordinated to a hierarchical and thematic ordering.

It would appear that the colleges were originally grouped in five sets of three: (1) Christ Church, New, Magdalen; (2) All Souls, Corpus Christi, Merton; (3), Oriel, Queen's, University College; (4) Brasenose, Lincoln, Exeter; (5) Trinity, Balliol, St John's, with each group separated by a brief passage of linking dialogue. The first three colleges are, in fact, physically distant from each other, but these were the largest and most prestigious foundations. Christ Church, as the royal foundation, naturally comes first, followed by New College and Magdalen, the two next largest, wealthiest and architecturally most magnificent foundations. The succeeding group comprises the three foundations next in order of rank.[22] From this point, the succession of colleges does appear to follow a more explicitly topographical order, ending with a group of three colleges lying outside the city walls. Even here, this last grouping is endowed with thematic significance, introduced by the text as a set of colleges founded by laymen.

The fitting *colophon*, or crowning touch, to the sequence is provided by the double-page spread of the Schools, or lecture rooms, both linked with royal patronage. The Divinity School, the most magnificent building of the university, was associated with Humfrey, Duke of Gloucester, a son of Henry IV; the Public Schools, the lecture rooms devoted to the arts and philosophies, had recently been rebuilt from a bequest by Queen Mary. These are the last buildings to be provided with illustrations and effectively complete the itinerary. The description of the Halls, or hostels, provides a coda to the tour. Hart Hall, where Neale himself was resident, is given a whole verse to itself and the remaining eight are are collected together in a brief epitome, although their names are given some visual distinction by being underlined in red ink (fol. 18).[23]

Neale's dialogue, with its accompanying pictures, though undoubtedly intended as a delightful and entertaining conceit couched in the character of a courtly conversation, clearly had a larger purpose and a specific moral and political theme. The itinerary described presents the topographical description of Oxford as a moralized history, in which each college founder, whether monarch, bishop, ecclesiastic or layman, is eulogized as an exemplar of beneficent patronage directed to the advancement of learning.

The treatment of Exeter College provides a particularly pointed example of this theme. Although Bereblock's drawing shows this to have been architecturally the least distinguished of the colleges, it is given great prominence in the dialogue by being made the prompt for an extended discussion of patronage in general, and lay patronage in particular (fols. 13–13^{v}). The Queen's exclamation on the virtue of its episcopal founders, '*O Pia pontificum mens haec*' ('O, how devout are the minds of prelates'), leads into the Chancellor's long eulogy of Sir William Petre, one of the Queen's most trusted Privy Councillors, who had only recently completed the arrangements for a grand benefaction to the college.[24] Petre is presented as the exemplar of the desired moral effect of the dialogue, and more generally, as evidence of Oxford's, and the nation's, good fortune under the 'happy reign' of Elizabeth (who had assisted Petre in establishing his benefaction). Bereblock himself had been one of the first appointees to the new Petrean Fellowships, only a few months before the Royal Visit, and, appropriately, it is at this point in the dialogue that his authorship of the drawings is advertised, Neale presenting him in turn as the exemplar of the fruits of the patron's munificence:

> How great the students are that this place produces
> for you, the rest of the crowd can learn from this
> one individual. That man will be Bereblock, whose
> most dexterous right hand created these images
> with marvellous dexterity.[25]

St John's College, the last, and youngest, of the colleges, that had been recently founded by the London merchant Sir Thomas White, is also given special treatment with an additional introductory verse, and a pretty compliment, where Leicester describes it as the beloved 'Benjamin' of his colleges. As with the treatment of Petre, this is also an act of filial piety on behalf of the authors, both of whom, in this case, had benefited from White's patronage.[26]

It is the activities of royal patrons, however, which are of greatest import in the dialogue, particularly those of Elizabeth's father, Henry VIII, the founder of Christ Church, and her sister, Queen Mary I, patron of the rebuilt Schools. This celebration of previous acts of patronage is couched as a barely disguised appeal to the Queen to follow their example, to emulate her father, her sister and the founders of the past, and to continue to pledge further spiritual and material support to the university. The Chancellor's peroration concludes with the eulogy of Elizabeth herself, as the heir and finisher of her father's generosity, summed up in the alliterative line, underlined in red for added emphasis, *'Patrizans Patri par pietate pari'* ('taking after your father, equal your father's equal devotion') (fol. 19).

Neale and his contemporaries would have been only too aware of the content of the Queen's farewell speech delivered on her visit to Cambridge two years before, in which she had spoken of the many fine buildings she had seen, the monuments of their famous founders, and held out the vague promise that she too would one day 'leave some famous monument behind me'.[27] The hope that she would make the same promise to Oxford is only too evident in the argument of Neale's verse.

Neale's decision to cast his dialogue as an imaginary journey may also be related to the example of the Cambridge visit. On that occasion the Queen had undertaken an actual progress round each of the colleges, an event associated with a textual accompaniment, intended for presentation to the Queen. In advance of the visit Sir William Cecil, her Chief Secretary and Chancellor of Cambridge University, had ordered the university to make a book containing a digest of all 'the founders and benefactors of every college' together with a book containing all the gratulatory verses composed for the Queen. On the day of the progress, Cecil 'caried the bookes in his owne handes and at everye colledge pervsed the same'.[28] The book of founders is suggestive as an initial model for Neale's Topographical Delineation (might Cecil have read from it to the Queen as they rode around the colleges?), but here the task has been accomplished with significantly greater flourish and invention, transforming the prose catalogue into an occasion of poetic performance and made an object of especial delight through its drawings.

There may even have been a more pressing context for the conception of the illustrated dialogue. On the Oxford visit there was to be no progress around the individual colleges as there had been at Cambridge. How far in advance of the visit this decision became known is unclear, but it may well have been the case that the Topographical Delineation was conceived not simply as a 'virtual progress', but as a *substitute* for a progress: an alternative means of keeping before the Queen's eyes a memorable image of Oxford, and of its exemplary benefactors, long after the visit had ended.[29] The collective encomium, or praise, of the founders of the past, is an exhortation to future action.

The exhortation was in keeping with the political tenor of the occasion. The Royal Visits to Oxford and Cambridge in the early years of the Queen's reign had a distinct agenda: to ensure conformity of the universities to the policies of the new regime, but also to cultivate and strengthen them as allies and as the training grounds for the next generation of loyal servants. The Queen's speech at Cambridge was received as a declaration of intent to this end, and Neale's exhortation acts both as a compliment to and recognition of that policy, as well as a reminder that Oxford hoped to share in the benefits as much as Cambridge.[30]

BEREBLOCK THE DRAUGHTSMAN

Only rarely does Neale attempt passages of architectural description in his text, the notable exception being his verse on the Divinity School, where the whole is given over to celebration of its architecture, marvelling at its 'innumerable towers' and its splendid vault which 'glitters in the light from the abundant windows'. The task of praising the buildings is, rather, accomplished through the 'visual rhetoric' of Bereblock's pictures. It will be necessary to examine these drawings in more detail, not least because they have sometimes been misunderstood as naive or as deficient in perspective, a viewpoint informed, no doubt, by an implied comparison with David Loggan's magisterial engravings of the Oxford colleges, published in the late seventeenth century (Fig. 1).[31] In place of such anachronistic readings, it will be more productive to consider them as a product of sixteenth-century visual concerns and practices.

Bereblock must have already enjoyed some reputation in Oxford as an accomplished scribe, for in 1562, he had been chosen to write

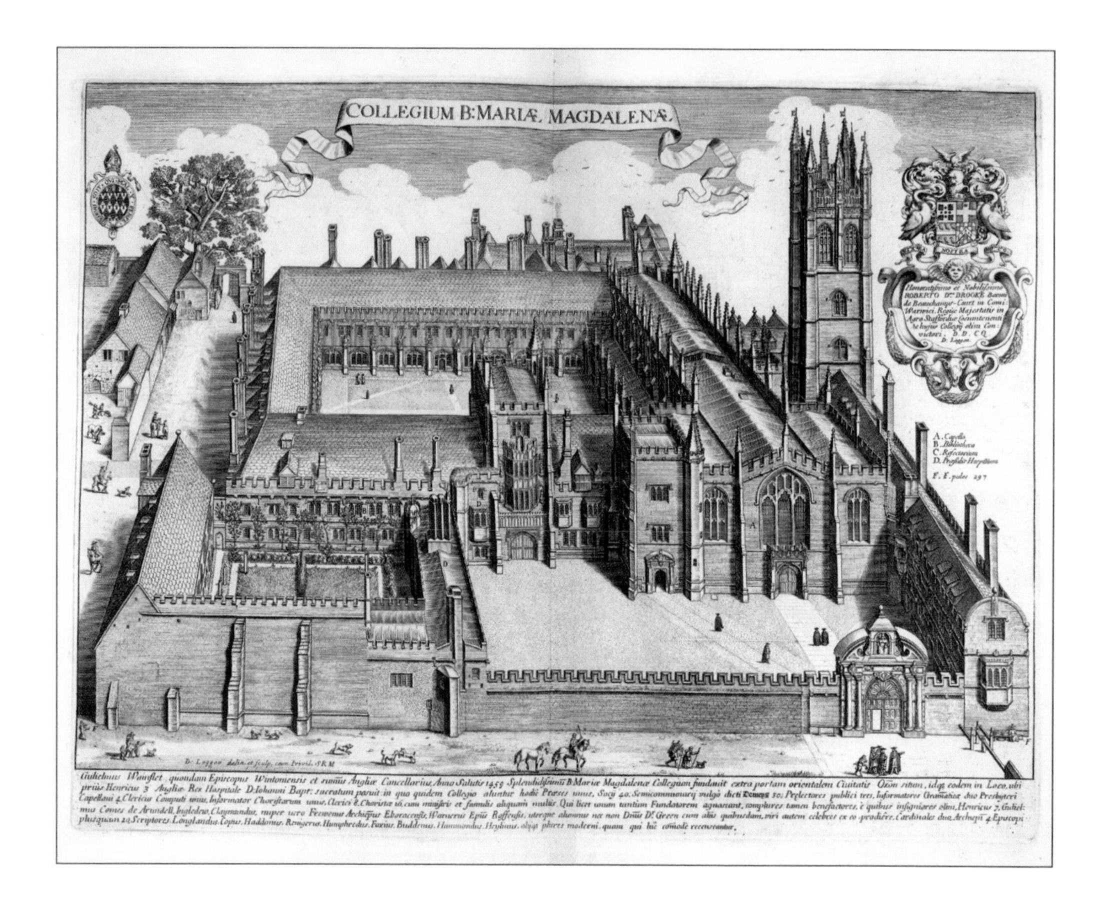

Fig. 1: *Magdalen College* David Loggan, Oxonia Illustrata, (Oxford, 1675).

out the new book of Statutes for St John's College where he was then a Fellow. The title page, which he enriched with a miniature of the Trinity and a carefully worked rendering of the founder's arms, demonstrates his skill as a draughtsman as well as a calligrapher (Fig. 2). His signature, 'John Berblock Scriptor', appears at the foot of the page and his name is worked into some of the elaborate calligraphic initial letters provided for each chapter.[32] His skill as a miniaturist is even more evident in the finely detailed architectural drawings of the Queen's Book. He achieves an extraordinary density in these images through very close hatching of surfaces, suggestive of shading and texture, and through increasing intensity of the drawing where he attempts to convey the effects of sculptural enrichment. The heraldic beasts on the gatehouse range at Christ Church (fol. 5v) provide a particularly good example of his concern for closely observed detail, and he takes great delight in rendering the visual effects of the pinnacles, such as those at Merton and the Divinity School, whose crockets, worked in solid ink, seem to sparkle on the page like black jewels (fols. 7ᵛ, 16ᵛ).

One of the most striking features of the series of drawings, when seen as a whole, is their uniformity of presentation, a controlled ordering that argues against any notion of naivety. The visual experience gained from turning the carefully designed pages of this manuscript is that of a stately procession of regular buildings. Bereblock has adopted a consistent formula for his pictures. In a manner which bears a striking analogy with contemporary portrait painting, where the subject was often represented against an abstract blue background (Fig. 3), Bereblock presents the particular 'physiognomy' of each of his colleges and buildings as if abstracted from its setting, eschewing any indications of such contingent factors as adjoining buildings, landscapes, skyscapes or even cast shadows, except where those shadows are conveying information about the surfaces of the buildings themselves.

Fig. 2:
Statutes of St John's College, Oxford. John Bereblock, 1562. Title page.

The construction of each drawing is also carefully controlled. Each is framed within co-ordinate lines against which the diagonals of the receding ranges and the horizontals of the frontal faces are plotted, and within this framework the drawings have then been built up with freehand drawing of windows and architectural detail. When dealing with the larger, regular buildings, however, such as the hall of Christ Church (fol. 5ᵛ) or the Divinity School (fol. 16ᵛ), the spacing of the window bays has been plotted by rule, rather than drawn in freely. In the majority of the college drawings the gatehouse range is rendered more or less frontally with the side ranges treated in parallel, or diverging, perspective. In the drawings of Corpus Christi and All Souls (fols. 7, 9ᵛ), however, the upper stages of the gate tower are given a radically different orientation from the base, not through naivety or clumsiness, but, it would seem, in order to incorporate the representation of important windows on the opposite

Fig. 3: *Richard Fox, Bishop of Winchester.* Joannes Corvus, 1530–2? Corpus Christi College, Oxford.

range of the quadrangle. The most exuberant example of this 'additive' approach can be seen in the image of Magdalen College (fol. 8^{v}), where the spatial complexity of the drawing seems to be a response to the multiple foci of architectural magnificence within this part of the college complex.

It is this tendency to treat each architectural volume of the building as a separate entity, rather than to subordinate the whole to a single viewpoint, which has led some earlier commentators to undervalue Bereblock's drawings; yet this clearly arises from the consistent application of a different representational logic. These composite views are concerned with maximizing the information that can be conveyed about the particular visual experiences to be had from each building, particularly where it concerns the experience of scale, of richly carved stone and of expensive glazing.

He also abbreviates or summarizes aspects of the buildings he represents. The drawing of Merton College, for example, may be in one sense 'inaccurate' in representing the main body of the chapel as a four-bayed rather than a seven-bayed structure, but his rendering of it conveys, rather, an epitome of its magnificence and a vivid sense of its overwhelming scale relative to the other buildings of the college. This drawing also demonstrates another of his emphases, a concern for effects of great height. The pinnacles of the chapel tower here, as also in the drawing of Magdalen, extend beyond the upper frame line. While this suggestive device may simply be the happy consequence of a misjudgement on Bereblock's part, his treatment of the pinnacles in the All Souls drawing (fol. 9^{v}), where the farther pinnacles of the chapel 'disappear' behind the frame line, suggests instead a self-conscious, and even witty, manipulation of his representational means.

We can identify a similar combination of generalization and particularization in the treatment of surfaces and textures through the systematic application of a set of graphic conventions. Traceried windows are indicated through a schematic shorthand notation, glazed and unglazed openings are differentiated with either a diamond-shaped network, suggestive of leading, or a rectilinear gridding, suggestive of iron bars or wooden louvres. Distinctions between leaded and tiled roofs are carefully maintained, the latter represented by a characteristic fish-scale pattern, the former represented by smooth hatching. These distinctions convey, of course, not only visual information, but information about the relative costliness of the materials employed.

Bereblock undoubtedly took preparatory studies of the buildings on the spot, taking care to observe their particular beauties as well as their topographical peculiarities. The rich panelling of the gate tower at Brasenose (fol. 11v), for example, is made a focus of attention, whereas in the representation of New College, where the college gate is set within the confines of a narrow lane, Bereblock dispenses with his customary gatehouse view altogether. He has selected instead an equally imaginary viewpoint from beyond the city walls, a view that afforded the most spectacular prospect of the rich fenestration and elaborate pinnacles of the chapel and hall.

Clearly, then, these drawings were intended as 'portraits' of their subjects and not as generalized types. As with portraiture, however, accommodations have been made between the demands of record and the demands of decorum. The very obvious shifts in scale between different elements of the buildings serve to emphasize passages of architectural distinction: turreted towers and crocketed pinnacles are given great prominence and windows are uniformly overscaled and regularized.[33] Bereblock's representational method demonstrates just as much concern for magnificence as for veracity and it is in this respect that we can speak of the 'visual rhetoric' of the drawings and further consider how this echoes the rhetoric of the verses, which are also celebrations of 'magnificence'.

THE CHOROGRAPHICAL PORTRAIT

Parallels for aspects of Bereblock's additive and selective approach to representing buildings can certainly be found in later medieval practice, as for example in the drawings of Wells, Winchester College and New College, Oxford in the late fifteenth-century Chaundler manuscript (Fig. 4), but the consistency of approach is new.[34] Indeed, by describing their

Fig. 4:
New College, Oxford.
The 'Chaundler Manuscript', c.1464

work as a 'Topographical Delineation', Neale and Bereblock would seem to be self-consciously locating it within the context of newly-emergent forms of mapping, in particular, the contemporary vogue for bird's-eye view city maps (Fig. 5). This approach to mapping was developed in late fifteenth-century Italy, and by the mid-sixteenth century these city views, often titled 'portraits', 'topographies' or 'chorographies', were being produced in increasing numbers in Italy, France, Germany and the Low Countries, whether as separate images or as illustrations in printed books.[35] The fashion reached its zenith in the many volumes of Braun and Hogenberg's albums of city views, the *Civitates Orbis Terrarum,* published in Cologne between 1572 and 1617.

Bereblock's bird's-eye views of the buildings of Oxford may usefully be seen as presentations in microcosm of these new city views; indeed, as will be discussed below, he may even have made a map of Oxford in association with the book of drawings presented to the Queen. His work has not hitherto been recognized in this context but it demands to be seen as an important early example of the new 'map-consciousness' developing in England in the middle decades of the century.[36] The real expansion in English map-making was still to come, in the 1570s and beyond, and at this date very few Englishmen were actually practising as map-makers. The earliest known example of the new form of city view to be printed in England is the fine bird's-eye view of Norwich included in William Cuningham's *The Cosmographical Glasse* (1559), and printed views of London were also beginning to appear, in the late 50s and early 60s (Fig. 6).[37]

The Cosmographical Glasse, which Bereblock almost certainly knew, was an expensively produced and handsomely illustrated treatise on geography, astronomy and map-making.[38] The book had been dedicated to Lord Robert Dudley (the future Earl of Leicester), who is lauded in the dedicatory preface as a patron of mathematical and scientific scholarship. Leicester does seem to have had a genuine interest in maps and mapping, and it may be that that Neale and Bereblock's topographical work was calculated to be particularly appealing to their Chancellor.[39]

Cuningham's book attests to a contemporary concern for the intellectual value of visual representation and for the making of maps as an appropriate activity for a scholar.[40] The map of Norwich, which he himself had made, is presented in the text as a visual definition of 'chorography'. The term, a synonym for topography, was taken from the classical geographer Ptolemy, whose *Geographia* was a central text for the development of renaissance mapping. Ptolemy had defined chorography as the representation of particular places or regions, as differentiated from the abstract analysis of the world as a whole, which was the province of geography. For his early modern followers, like Cuningham, whose book is an important example of this diffusion of Ptolemaic concepts into the English vernacular, this activity was explicitly associated with a pictorial rather than mathematical mode of knowledge.[41]

The status of topography/chorography as a form of knowledge was the subject of lively debate in the mid-sixteenth century. For its detractors it was unscientific, concerned with the ephemeral qualities of sense percep-

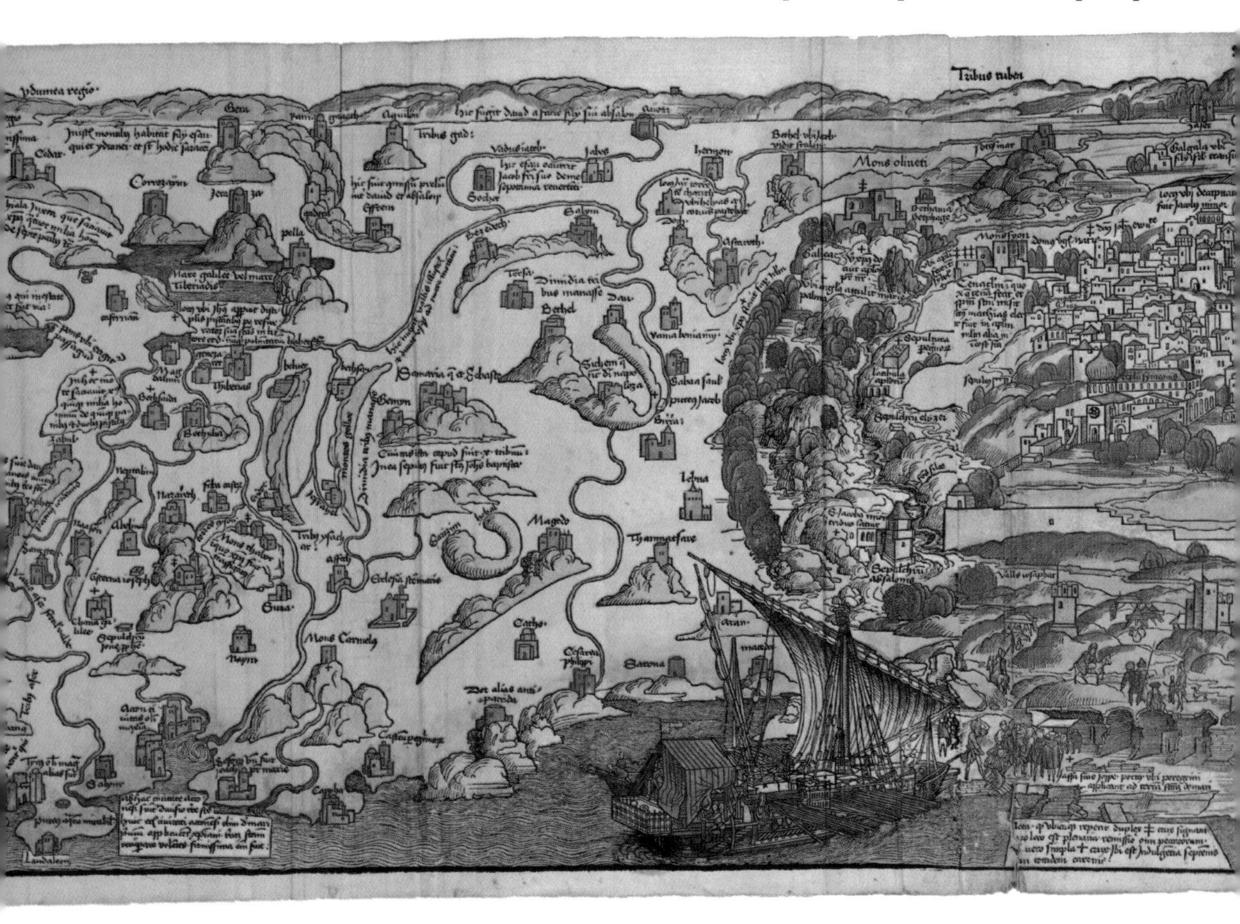

Fig. 5: *Jerusalem.* Bernhard von Breydenbach, *Peregrinatio in Terram Sanctam* (Mainz, 1486).

tion rather than with the abstract mathematical verities of cosmology; but its supporters developed arguments which stressed the superior veracity of the visual record, assembled from direct observation, and the capacity of the visual map to present, as if in one view, the knowledge of many views.[42] This synthetic approach to the representation of cities is evident in many of these early modern pictorial maps, as is their complex relationship to the issue of systematic measuring. Despite their seductively 'factual' appearance, these are highly constructed artefacts, assembled from views taken from a series of real or imaginary vantage points, in order to present a more comprehensive or 'truthful' portrait of the rich visual experience of the place being described. Strict perspectival representation, which would subject the image of the whole to the authority of a single viewpoint, was rarely attempted in these views, no doubt because the foreshortenings and

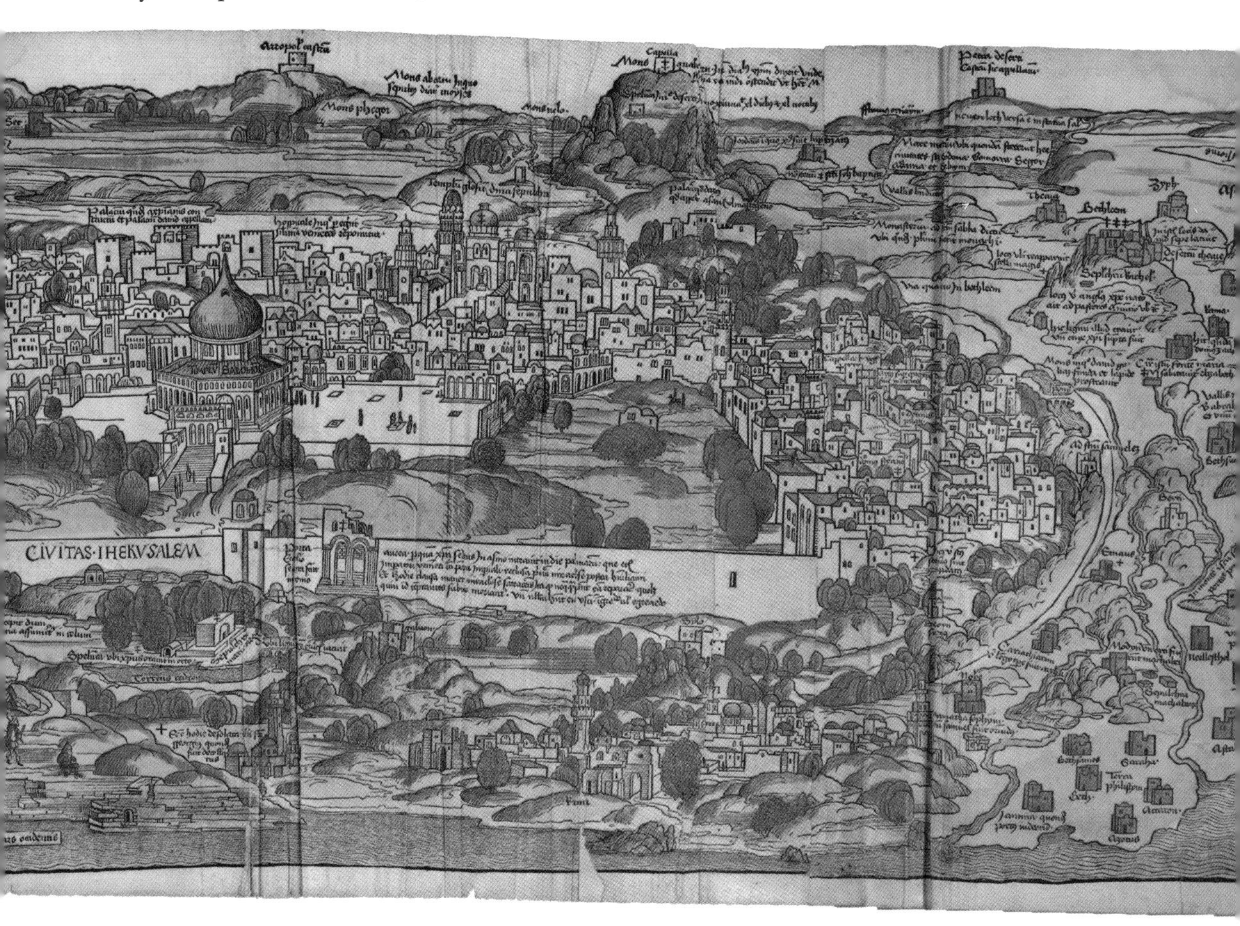

Fig. 6: Map of Norwich. WilliamCuningham, *The Cosmographical Glasse* (London, 1590).

distortions necessitated by such an approach were insufficient to portray the complexities of cityscape.[43]

Bereblock's Oxford drawings seem to have been produced from within the same set of visual habits, synthesizing multiple views of the buildings, within an appearance of systematic recording, in order to convey a satisfyingly 'lifelike' portrait of their particular visual qualities.[44] It is unfortunate that a map of Oxford, possibly made by Bereblock in 1566, from which a more detailed understanding of his approach to representation could be understood, has now been lost. This map of Oxford was displayed at the entrance to St Mary's Church for three days during the Royal Visit of 1566. Miles Windsor recorded its appearance in his account of the visit:

> As ye Queene entred ye churche, there were diverse
> shedes of verses in Latyn Greeke and Hebrew,
> sett upon ye doores & walles & a certayne mappe

> of Oxford made by Mr Neale [sic] describing
> ye colledges & halles wth verses underwritten
> & so was there on Wednesdaye & Thursdaye
> followinge.[45]

The attribution of the map to Neale underscores its association in Windsor's mind with the little book of the colleges and schools which he records Neale presenting to the Queen only a few paragraphs beforehand, though he was clearly unaware of Bereblock's involvement in its making. It is not quite clear what is being described here: perhaps the map was only a series of larger copies of the illustrated pages of the manuscript, arranged in successive sheets, rather than a view of the city. The account of the map by Nicholas Robinson, however, suggests that it was a city view.[46] It might be expected, from the evidence of the college drawings, that it would have attempted the high oblique perspective view employed in many of the newly fashionable city views, of the form adopted by Ralph Agas in his slightly later map of Oxford, drawn in 1578 and printed in 1588 (Fig. 7).[47]

The lost map of Oxford has been identified with a picture known to have been owned by St John's College in the early seventeenth century, the 'Grate Picture of the colleges ... which did usually hang in Mr. President's lodgings' recorded in the College Register for August 1616.[48] The picture, described as 'old worke', was clearly a desirable item since in that year Sir Thomas Lake, Secretary of State, had asked the college to make a present of it to him. His request was granted, but only in return for a sizeable donation of £20 towards the building works then in progress at the college.[49] Though Bereblock's name is not associated with the picture in this particular document, he is described in another St John's document of the same period as 'distinguished in the art of delineating, as many surviving maps show, especially the one of Rochester, drawn by him', but this map of Rochester, as well as the 'grate picture', has since been lost.[50]

How are we to understand the relationship between this lost map of Oxford and the book of drawings given to the Queen? Were the two conceived simultaneously, the book intended as a smaller 'souvenir' copy of the map, to be retained by the Queen for her private enjoyment?[51] Or did the idea of the map come first? It could be conjectured that it was

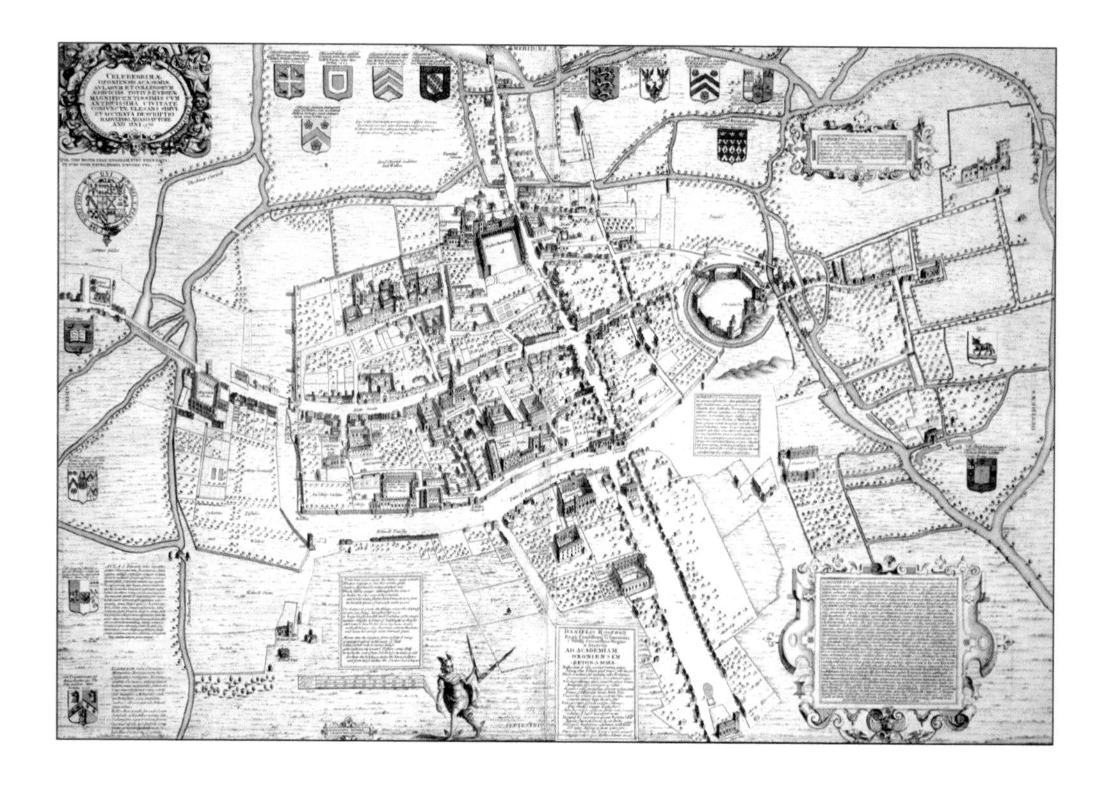

Fig. 7: *Map of Oxford.* Surveyed by Ralph Agas, 1578, engraved by Augustine Ryther, 1588. Rengraved by Robert Whittlesey, 1728. Detail.

already in preparation when it became known that the Queen would not be visiting all the colleges, and that this gave rise to the idea of adapting its components into another format, providing the Queen with another way of 'seeing' the colleges. The verses underneath the images certainly have a freestanding quality, easily detachable from the more private passages of dialogue within which they have been inserted, and this is indeed how they appear in a book published by Windsor in 1590. In his *Academiarum Catalogus,* a history of the universities of Europe, his section on Oxford concludes with a set of these verses. It could well be that this publication preserves the original text as it appeared on the map.[52]

The precise circumstances of the genesis of the book and the map cannot be established with certainty, but it is significant that in each case the pictures of the buildings are set within a framework of laudatory verse. Recent scholarship on the development of renaissance chorography has emphasized its rhetorical character, as a practice invested with meanings beyond empirical recording. These city views are rarely left to 'speak for themselves' but are literally overwritten with a textual apparatus of titles and text panels lauding the cities they represent. This is particularly visible in the Agas Map of Oxford, which has eight text panels, some in English, some in Latin, some in verse, some in prose, which collectively tell the history of the city and the university and celebrate its fame. In parallel with the textual encomium or praise, the detailed representation of the physical appearance of the city, in this and other city views of the period, functions as a 'visual encomium', in which the present view of the city epitomises the history of its coming into being and its present fame.[53]

It may seem a big leap to move from the great city views to Bereblock's small drawings, but these too function as visual encomia, analogous to the literary praise of the founders conducted in Neale's verse. The manuscript as a whole has been shaped within this emerging discourse of chorography, sharing those impulses of rhetorical celebration and historical particularizing that we find in the city maps of the period, though here it has been adapted to the needs of a very specific political occasion.[54]

THE EMBLEMATIC PORTRAIT

The chorographical maps of the period provide one important context for understanding the conception of Neale and Bereblock's Topographical Delineation, but the specific page-design adopted in their book suggests comparison with other contemporary genres of verbal-visual rhetoric. The illustrated pages echo the format of the epigram-portrait, an explicitly encomiastic type, in which the picture of the famous scholar or nobleman is addressed by a laudatory verse beneath. Portraits of this type were employed as title pages to printed books, as well as in painted portraits of the period, and by the later decades of the sixteenth century these were being collected into albums of 'famous men', notably in books such as Philipp Galle's *Virorum Doctorum de Disciplinis Benemerentium Effigies XLIIII* (Antwerp, 1572) (Fig. 8).[55] The format has a strong thematic relationship to the exemplary 'portraits' provided in the Queen's Book of Oxford, but there is a further new bimedial form of the period to which they

Fig. 8: *Ludovico Vives.* Philipp Galle, *Virorum Doctorum de Disciplinis Benemerentium Effigies* (Antwerp, 1572).

bear equally close comparison. The illustrated pages also bear a striking resemblance to the typographical formats adopted in contemporary emblem books, collections of moral precepts or proverbs illustrated through a combination of picture and verse.

The fashion for these was initiated with Andrea Alciato's *Emblematum Liber* published in 1531, and its formula of motto, image and verse was developed, codified, and expanded in later editions and in the publications of numerous followers (Fig. 9). As with the epigram-portrait, the analogy to be drawn here is not only visual but also thematic. The emblem presented its readers with the exemplification of a moral precept or commonplace, which they were invited to decipher through pondering the meaning of the verse and picture and the relationship between them. In the Topographical Delineation the moral addressed in the verses is not illustrated by an allegorical device or enigmatic picture, but by a portrait, that of a building.[56]

The 'emblematic' character of the Topographical Delineation is announced by the 'frontispiece' to the manuscript, which shares the same page layout as those on which the buildings are illustrated, and itself takes the form of an emblem: the *Hebraismi Typus,* or image of Hebrew Learning, represented by a flourishing tree (fol. iiv). Tree emblems were popular in contemporary emblem books, but the signification of this tree, as expanded by its accompanying verse, is not generic but specific to place and person. It is intended as a compliment to royal munificence, and celebrates the endowment of the Regius Professorship of Hebrew, 'planted' by Henry VIII in Oxford and 'watered' by his successor, Elizabeth.[57] By extension, the emblem also refers to Neale himself, the current holder of the Professorship, who offers dutifully the fruits of his learning as a gift to the 'Royal Gardener'.[58] This emblem is clearly intended to be read as integral to the text as a whole, since its themes are recapitulated

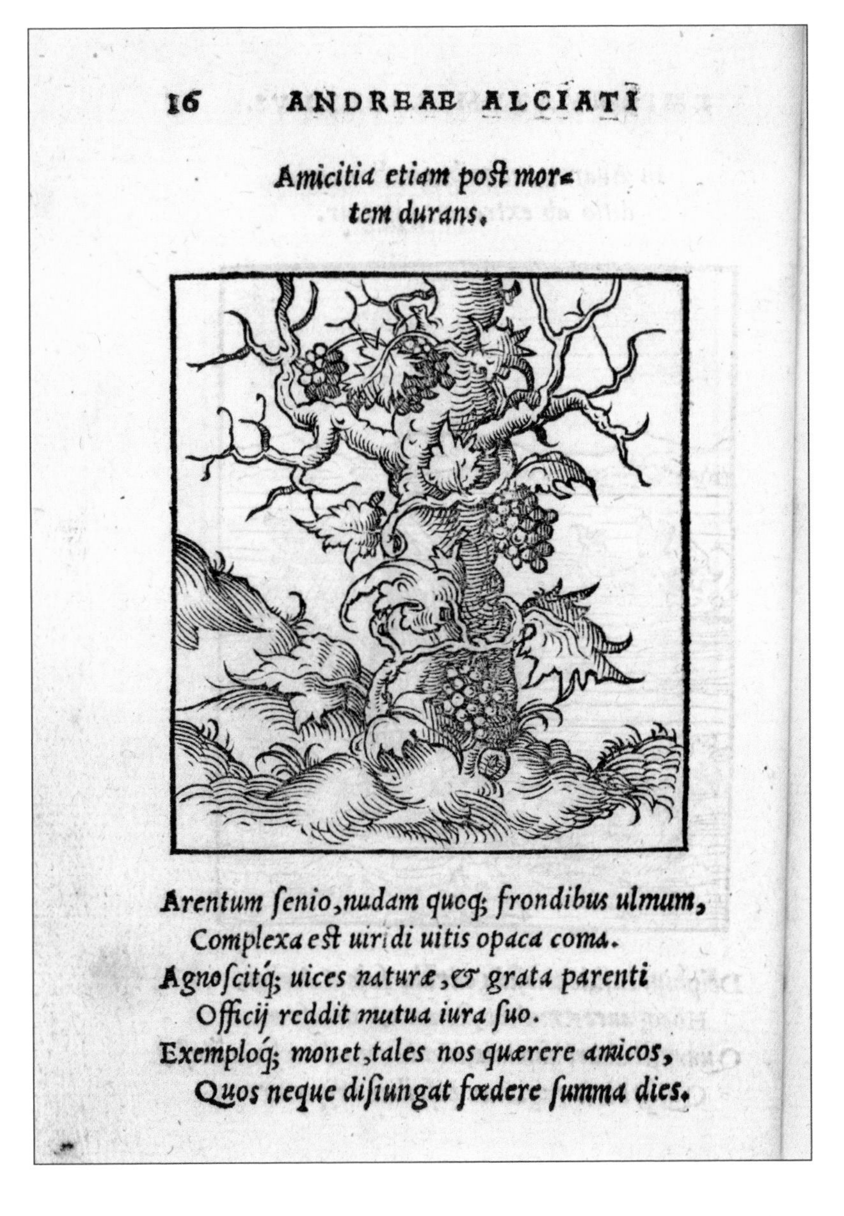

16 ANDREAE ALCIATI

Amicitia etiam poſt mortem durans.

Arentum ſenio,nudam quoq; frondibus ulmum,
Complexa eſt uiridi uitis opaca coma.
Agnoſcitq; uices naturæ,& grata parenti
Officij reddit mutua iura ſuo.
Exemploq; monet,tales nos quærere amicos,
Quos neque diſiungat fœdere ſumma dies.

Fig. 9:
'Amicitia etiam post mortem durans.'
Andrea Alciato,
Emblematum Libellus
(Paris, 1534).

in the closing lines of the dialogue. Here Leicester, in the voice of the Chancellor, employs the same tree metaphor in addressing the Queen as the heir to and finisher of her father's patronage and, indeed, concludes his discourse by introducing Neale himself as the 'fruitful tree' waiting to present his gift to his sovereign (fol. 19). It may not be coincidental that the actual presentation of the manuscript seems to have taken place in the gardens at Christ Church, suggesting, perhaps, a conscious staging of the event in keeping with the thematic of the emblem.[59]

This may not have been the first occasion on which Bereblock collaborated on the production of an emblematic text, nor, indeed, on a text intimately associated with the Earl of Leicester. He may well have been involved in the making of the earliest known English emblem book, Thomas Palmer's 'Two Hundred Poosees', a manuscript collection of emblems probably made in Oxford 1565/6 and dedicated to Leicester.[60] John Manning has suggested that he may have been responsible for the twenty-one hand-drawn pictures appearing in this manuscript, two of which are signed with monogram 'IB'. Most of the remaining pictures were actually cut out of printed emblem books, from France and Flanders, and pasted directly onto the pages. Palmer, like Bereblock, had been a fellow of St John's College in the early 1560s, where he was the college's first lecturer in Rhetoric, and the two men would have known each other well. This proximity, together with the evidence of his work on the college statutes, informed Manning's view of Bereblock as a likely candidate for the role of Palmer's illustrator.[61] The identification here of the *Hebraisimi Typus* emblem as Bereblock's work, and a comparison of the style of the Palmer drawings with those of the Oxford buildings, which show similarities in handling, further strengthens the case for his role in the 'Two Hundred Poosees'.[62] If the Palmer drawings are indeed Bereblock's work then we can be sure that he would have had significant knowledge of continental emblems books, judging by the range of texts from which the pasted-in images were culled.[63]

In view of Bereblock's precocious involvement in emblem making and of the 'emblematic' character of the Queen's Book itself, it would now seem misleading to call Neale's verses on the colleges 'descriptions', as is often the case.[64] In place of the 'topoi' of rhetoric, the commonplaces made to reveal moral truths, here actual 'places' are rendered significant: topos and topography unite and each college founder, through the buildings that act as their 'portraits', becomes an exemplar of the virtues of piety and munificence.

Queen Elizabeth probably saw very little of Oxford during the six days of her visit in the late summer of 1566. Apart from Christ Church, where she set up temporary court for the duration, she would have seen only the buildings passed on the way to and from St Mary's, to attend the disputations there, and would have caught a passing glimpse of the street fronts and skylines of St John's, Magdalen, All Souls and University colleges as she made her entrance and took her leave of the city. The splendours of the Divinity School remained unseen.

Neale and Bereblock's little book provided her with a novel substitute for the actual experience of the architectural riches of the city. As she turned the pages of the manuscript she could, in imagination, take possession of her university, marshalled as an orderly and harmonious procession of stately buildings, an image of an orderly and harmonious commonwealth of learning. The moral argument of the text, as a *dialogus gratulatorius*, complemented her and her counsellors' avowed policy of supporting the Universities, at the same time as exhorting her to deliver on those promises. But this moralized topography of Oxford was conceived in a form which would render it a delight, for the eyes and the intellect. Fashioned out of a fluid and flexible conflation of the most up-to-date cultural fashions, it combined the courtly courtesies of the dialogue form with the latest developments in mapping, and emblematics, complementing the Queen's own familiarity with these tropes and allusions.

Such, at least, must have been the intention and the hope. What happened to the little book after it was delivered into her hands we cannot know for certain. Perhaps it remained with Leicester, whose presence in the text is as important as her own. Whatever its eventual fate, Neale and Bereblock's book, developed in response to the circumstances of a specific political occasion, stands as a remarkable invention in a new experimental genre. Whether it is described as versified chorography, emblematic topography or illustrated encomium, or, indeed all three at once, there is very little else to compare with it in early Elizabethan England.

NOTE ON THE MANUSCRIPT

MS. Bodl. 13 Part A i–iv, 1–21.
Bodleian Library *Summary Catalogue,* no. 3056
190 x 143 mm, in a vellum binding of seventeenth-century date.
Donation inscription records the gift to the library by John More in 1630.

Bound with two other items (omitted from this facsimile), some time after 1630, possibly after 1634: (a) fols. 22–31: an early sixteenth-century copy on parchment of a Latin address by Bishop John Fisher, given before Henry VII in Cambridge in 1506; (b) fols. 32–61 (paper): collections of Psalms translated into in Italian verse, with dedicatory letter to Sir Thomas Bodley from Alberico Gentile, dated Oxford, New Year's Day 1581. Inscribed 'given to the library in Oxford fou[nded] by Sr Tho. Bodley, by Mr Laure[nce]Bodley sometime fellow of Exceter C[ollege] and Bachelor of Divinite'. Laurence Bodley, nephew of Sir Thomas, vacated his fellowship at Exeter in 1632 and died in 1634.

The facsimile reproduction follows the current order of the leaves in the manuscript (omitting blanks) and their folio numbers. The internal evidence of the text, and the evidence of other contemporary copies which follow a different order, suggests that this was not its original structure. This textual evidence suggests the following original sequence: (i is different paper), ii, (iii is an inserted slip), iv, 1, 2, 3, 4, 5, 8, 9, 7, 6, 10, 11, 12, 13, 14, 15, 16, 17, 18, 19, 20, 21. The present state of the manuscript makes it difficult to be certain of the codicological evidence. The following leaves appear still to be conjoint: fols. iv and 1, 4 and 5, 9 and 10, 12 and 13, 16 and 17, 18 and 21, and 19 and 20. These remaining bifolia, together with the watermark evidence (a pot of the type found in Briquet, 12464-12911), are consistent with the conjecture of an original structure made up of quires each containing four leaves (two bifolia), as follows: I (fols. ii, iv, 1, 2); III (fols. 9, 7, 6, 10); IV (fols. 11-14); VI (fols. 18-21). This leaves problems with quires II and V. Quire II (fols. 3, 4, 5, 8) cannot have formed a regular quire in the original structure: fols. 4 and 5 are conjoint, but fols. 3 and 8 never were. It remains possible that fols. 3 and 8 were always single leaves. Quire V is left with only three leaves (fols. 15-17). Fols. 16 and 17 are conjoint, but fol. 15 does not connect to anything, and there is no loss of text between fols. 17 and 18. Perhaps fol. 15 was also originally a single leaf.

COPIES

1. Miles Windsor, *Academiarum Quae Aliquando Fuere Et Hodie Sunt in Europa, Catalogus & Enumeratio Breuis* (London, 1590), STC 25841. Contains at 42–8, 'Chronographia sive Origo Collegiorum Oxoniensis Academiae, una cum descriptione eorundem, ad serenissimam Elisabetham Angliae, Franciae, Hyberniae reginam scripta 1566', a version of the verses and the notes on names and dates of founders which appear on the illustrated pages of the manuscript, together with the verses on the halls. The verses relating to Exeter and St John's colleges show significant variants from those in MS. Bodl. 13, with lines removed and new lines inserted. The whole may have been copied from an associated map of Oxford made by Neale and Bereblock, now lost, (see *26*–27 above) rather than from a copy of the complete text.

2. Bodl. MS. Twyne 21, 779–92. 'Dialogus in adventum Serenissimae Reginae Dominae Elisabethae gratulatorius...'. Contains a close version of the text only of fols. 4–19: it omits the frontispiece, dedicatory preface and the Hebrew verse and oration. The prose notes on the founders are collected together separately at fols. 789–92 as 'Epitome Chronographia Collegiorum Academiae Oxoniensis'. Date and hand uncertain. In addition to minor variants, this includes, at fol. 786, an additional six lines on St John's College, not appearing in MS. Bodl. 13 or in Windsor (1590).

PUBLICATION HISTORY

The manuscript (omitting the Hebrew oration and verse) was first published by Thomas Hearne as an appendix to his *Henrici Dodwelli De Parma Equestri Woodwardiana Dissertatio* (Oxford 1713), illustrated with reproductions of the original drawings. The drawings were reproduced again, in inaccurate and embellished form, as a border to Robert Whittelsey's *Oxonia Antiqua Instaurata,* a re-engraving of Ralph Agas's sixteenth-century map of Oxford. The text, unillustrated, was reproduced from the Hearne publication in both the first and second editions of John Nichols, *The Progresses and Public Processions of Queen Elizabeth* (1788; 1823) and again in C. Plummer (ed.), *Elizabethan Oxford: Reprints of Rare Tracts* (Oxford, 1887), 151–68. A 'photozincographic' facsimile of the complete manuscript, with a preface by Falconer Madan, was privately published in 1882 under the title *Collegiorum Scholarumque Publicarum Academiae Oxoniensis, Topographica Delineatio* (Oxford, 1882).

THE MANUSCRIPT

Aspicis, ut uiget hæc fixis radicibus arbor?
Hâc illâc patulis frondibus aucta suis?
Arbor hebraismi typus est, quæ frondibus auctam
Se gaudet nummis, Elisabetha, tuis.
Plantauit Deus hanc primus sator in Paradiso.
Verbaq; mortales iussit hebræa loqui.
Transtulit hûc olim Pater hanc tuus inclytus, eius
Tu pia radices, Elisabetha, rigas.
Par est ergô tibi fructus hos proferat arbor,
Sumptibus, (ô Princeps maxima) culta tuis.

SERENISSIMÆ AVGVSTISSIMÆQVE PRINCIPI
Dominæ Elisabethæ Reginæ Angliæ, Franciæ
et Hiberniæ, Christianæ fidei pro=
pugnatrici &c. fausta
fæliciaque sunto
omnia.

HABES en (illustrissima Princeps Elisabetha) Oxo
niensis Academiæ tuæ Collegiorum scholarumque publica
rum qualemcumque topographicam delineationem, talem
partim scriptorio, partim carmine poëtico sub Dialogi
forma utrumque expressam, eius ut universam imagine
præsentem, quasique ob oculos expositam, pro tuo arbitratu
habeas, cuius incolæ bonarum artium omnium studios
sub auspicatissimo hoc regno tuo, haud aliter ac sub
Minervæ cuiusdam clypeo tuti, ardentius nihil obni
iusue à deo opt. max. contendunt, quam ut omnes a
singuli suam tibi, quam summa debent, observantiam
fidem, industriam certatim præstare possint. Cu
quidem delineandæ ratio tametsi crassiore quadam
Minerva & impolitiore tum stilo, tum carmine cons
quàm ut regiæ Ma.tis tuæ aspectu digna videri pos
dabis tamen (ut spero) veniam primis his re conati
in re noua. qui non alio, quàm gratulandi animo
serenissimæ Maiestatis tuæ quam exoptatissimo huic i
nos adventui instituti sunt. Illud vero in univers

quâm fieri potest humillimè supplex regiam Maiestatem
tuam rogatam uelim (Princeps augustiss.) vt quæ
=pictoribus atque poëtis
Quidlibet audendi semper fuit æqua potestas,
eam mihi nequaquam hîc interclusam esse velis. interea tem=
poris dum regiæ Maiestatis tuæ nomini amplissimo Dia=
logi partem alteram interlocutoriam attribuo, alteram verò
honoratiss.o Domino Roberto Dudlæo, Comiti Lecestrensi
nostroque Cancellario dignissimo vicissim accommodo. serua=
to tamen vtrobique (quod spero) vtriusque tùm tuæ, tum illius
personæ decoro. Argumentum porrò Dialogi tale fingitur,
quale ex abrupto, vel è re nata desumptum videri possit:
perinde ac si te (Regina nobilissima) Woodstochio disces=
suram Cancellarius interrogaret, et quò tandem profi=
cisci luberet, ut ex eo arrepta deinceps occasione, futuræ
narrationi topographicæ via quasi sterni videatur. Quæ si
Regiæ tuæ vnius præstantiæ quoquo modo grata esse poterit,
eadem tùm alijs multo gratior, tùm mihi quoque qualiscunque
hæc opera quam gratissima fuerit. Faxit deus opt. max.
ut quam diutissime valeas.

Serenissa Matis tuæ obsequentissimus
Alumnus, Thomas Neeus. hebraicæ
linguæ Professor Oxon.

[1r]

Dialogus in aduentum Reginæ serenissimæ
Dominæ Elisabethæ, gratulatorius, inter
eandem Reginam & Dominu Robertum
Dudlæum Comitem Lecestriæ & Oxonien=
sis Academiæ Cancellarium.

4

Interloquuntur REGINA & CANCELLARIUS OXON.

Cantell. SICCINE (chara tuis, regniq; columna Britanni
Elisabetha) domo pergis abire tua?

Regina. Non ego pergo domo peregre procul hospes abire,
Sed quo pergo, mea est Vrbs ea tota domus.

Cantell. Quod res est loqueris, (Princeps ter maxima,) tota
Nam regni sedes est domus ista tua.

Regina Quum sint ergo domus mihi plures, pluraq; tecta,
Quid ni mutarem tecta subinde mea?

Cantell. Sed si pace tua liceat mihi scire, lubenter
Hoc equidem scirem quo tibi tendat iter.

Regina Oxonium versus pergo, Musisq; dicata
Tecta peto, Musis concomitata meis.

Cantell. Et quæ tanta subit Musas ibi causa videndi,
Quum sit Musarum præsto caterua domi?

Regina Ipsamet illa domi Musarum præsto caterua
Has sibi sacratas suasit adire domos.

Cancell. Næ tu digna tuis persoluis præmia Musis.
Dum loca Musarum visere sacra paras.
Regina. Ecquid enimuero rerum spectabo nouarum?
Dignumve aduentu Principis ecquid habet?
Cancell. Vrbs antiqua tuis visenda patebit ocellis,
Et manibus ciues oscula fida dabunt.
Regina. Num quid præterea dignum aut memorabile cernam?
Quod merces tanto digna labore siet?
Cancell. Cernes præcipue Musarum quinque ter ædes,
Vrbs quibus Europæ non habet vlla pares.
Regina. Tune ergo has ædes nosti, quas Thamisis, amnis
Inclytus, alluuio cingit vtrinque suo?
Cancell. Quid ni pernoscam? quarum dux esse lubenter
Iam pridem cœpi, nec piget esse ducem.
Regina. Siccine tu subito Musis Dux esse volebas,
Qui Lecestrensis diceris esse Comes?

5

Cancell: Non minor est studijs, quam tas tris, fama praeesse,
Et Ducis et Comitis nomen vtrumque iuuat.
Regina. Quum harum breuiter mihi nomina pande domorum,
Quis, cui, quam, tulerit fautor & author opem.
Cancell. Hoc equidem faciam quanta breuitate licebit
Paucula metiri pluribus apta metris.

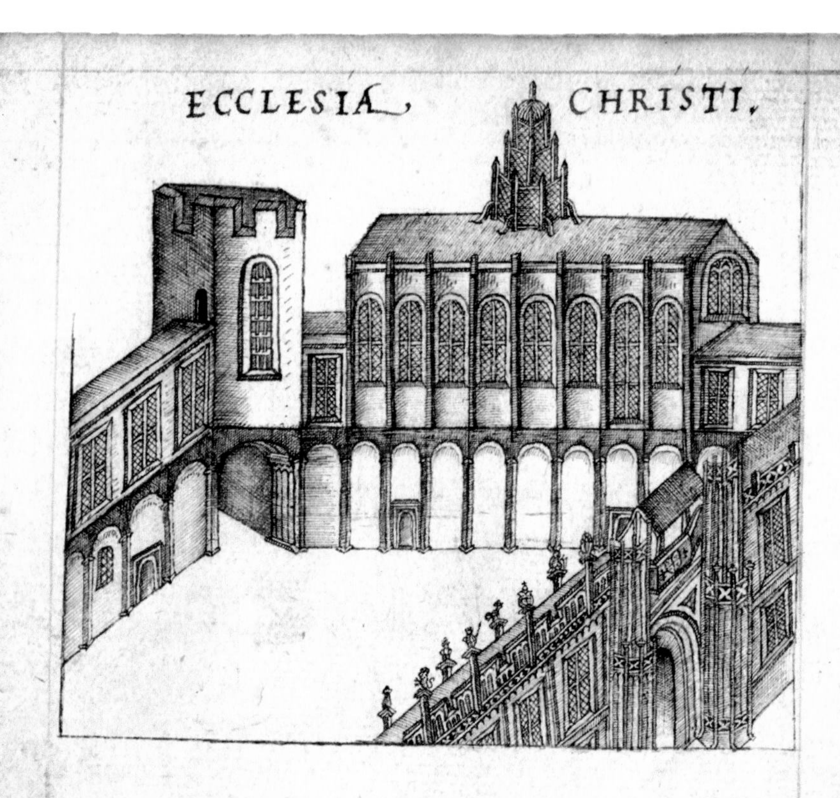

Prima stat australis Domus ampla, Ecclesia Christi,
Primo iam duplici nomine digna loco.
Tum quia te, patremque tuum sit nacta patronum,
Tum quia sit reliquis auctior ista cohors.
Cœpta quidem Thomæ Wulsæi sumptibus olim,
Sed patris Henrici censibus aucta tui.

Cœpit sub Henrico octauo. per Thomam Wulsæum Archiepiscopum Eboracensem. } Anno dni. 1529.
absoluta est ab eodem Henrico octauo. } Anno dni. 1546.

6

Regina interloquitur.

Regina. Vnde fit, vt, posset quum plures illa fouere,
Non foueat numeros vndiq; plena suos.
Cantell. Tot fouet illa quidem, quot par est census alendis.
Et plures aleret pluribus aucta bonis.
Inuida sed Musis mors immatura Patroni
Fecit, ut hii possit pluribus esse locus.
Regina. Est ergo cui quis possit prodesse: paratæ
Materiæ citius debita forma datur.

COLLEGIVM ORIALL.

antell.

Sed pergam in reliquis. stat Musis septima sedes
Orial, ô verè regia dicta domus.
Annis illa valens, Edwardi tempora vidit,
Qui rex illius nominis alter erat.
Condidit hanc Adam quidam cognomine Brownus,
Et regi nomen detulit ille suo.

Cœpit sub Edowardo secundo per dominū Adam Browne. Eleemosynarium eiusdem Edouardi Anno dñi 1323.

[6v]

COLLEGIUM CORPORIS CHRISTI. 7

Quinta iubet nostræ memores nos esse salutis.
Quo modo, & Vnde salus parta sit illa docens.
Quam Deus assumpto quia Christus corpore donat,
Corporis a Christi nomine nomen habet.
Censibus hanc amplis Richardus Foxus abunde
Sustinet, & Musis apta dat esse loca.

Cœpit sub Henrico Septimo per Richardum Fox. episcopum Wintoniensem. Anno dni } 1516°

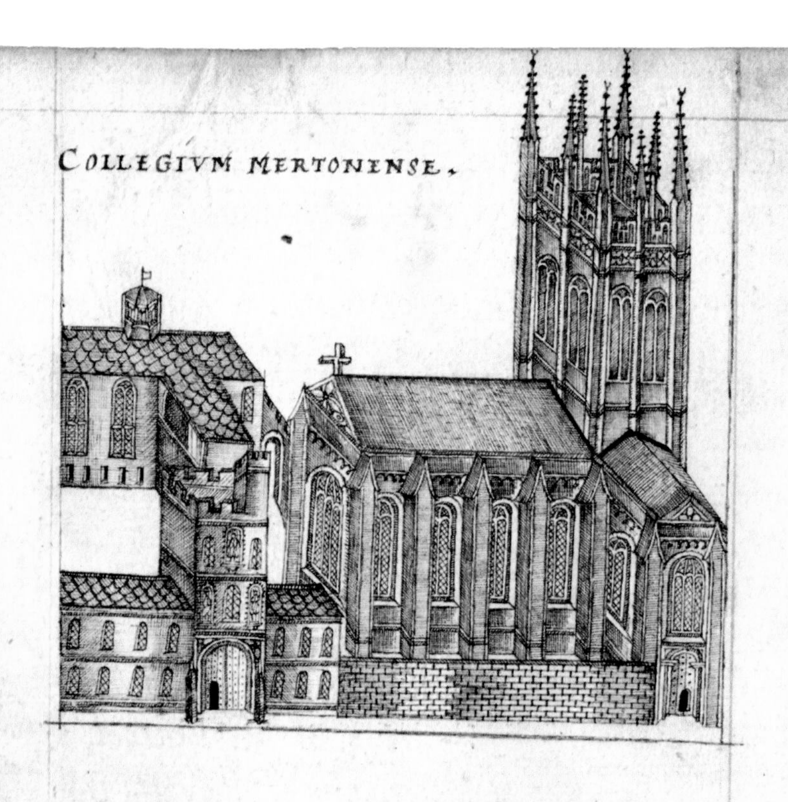

Nec procul hinc distat, quæ sexta est ordine Merton,
Seu Mertonensis dicta perampla Domus.
Gualterus Merton Præsul (quo Præsule Roffa
Floruit) huic Domui fautor & author erat.
Quæ quamuis multos foueat pia mater alumnos,
Ædes sacra tamen pluribus apta foret.

Cæpit sub Edouardo primo per Gualterum
Merton episcopum Roffensem. Anno dmi } 1276.

(1)

COLLEGIVM NOVVM.

Proxima mox sequitur satis ampla frequensq; studentū
Turba, noui cœtus nomen adepta diu.
Turribus hæc altis toto micat æthere, raris
Doctrinæ gemmis vitis onusta suis.
Condidit hanc Præsul Guilielmus, in vrbe wykama
Proles ter fausto sydere nata, Wykam.

Cœpit sub Richardo secundo per Guilielmū de Wykham
episcopum Wintoniensem. Anno dnī } 1375.

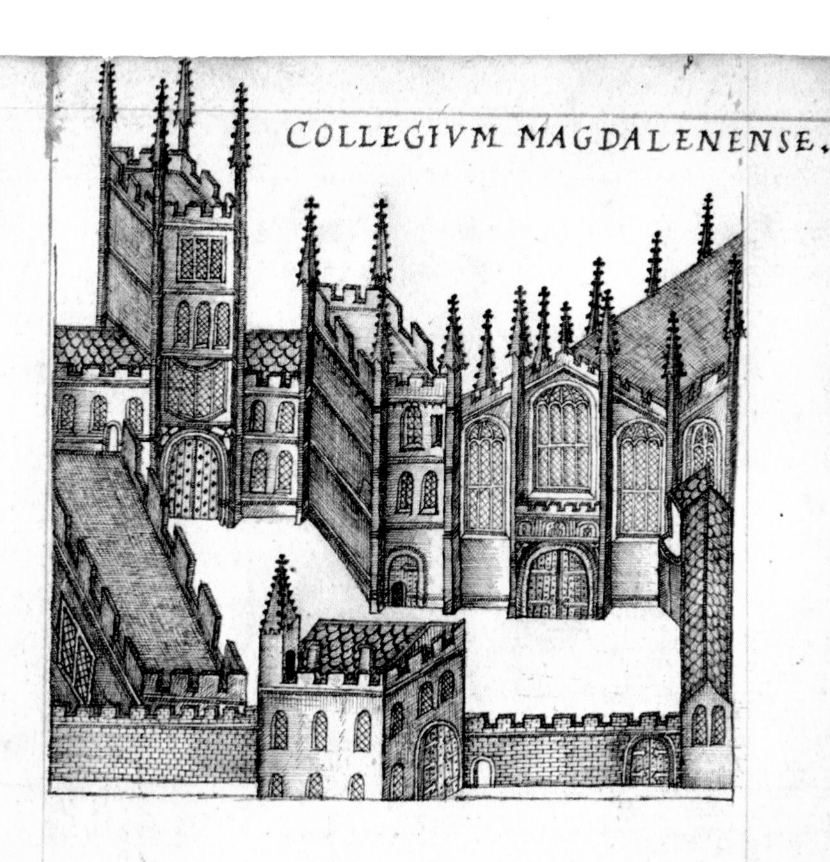

Nec minus est celebris domus ampla, dicata Mariæ,
Cuius sacra fidem Magdala castra docent,
Splendida munificum testantur tecta patronū,
Æmula splendoris digna, Wykame, tui.
Indidit huic nomen Guilielmus Waynflet, alumnus
Vnus & ipse gregis, magne Wykame, tui.

Cœpit sub Henrico sexto per Guilielmū Waynflet
episcopum Wintoniensem, Anno dn̄i. . . } 1459.°

9

Cancellarius interloquitur.

Cancell. Debebant paribus Collegia cætera verbis
Describi, mora ni tædia longa daret.

Regina. Perge modo. & reliquis data nomina prima recense,
Auribus hæc parient tædia nulla meis.

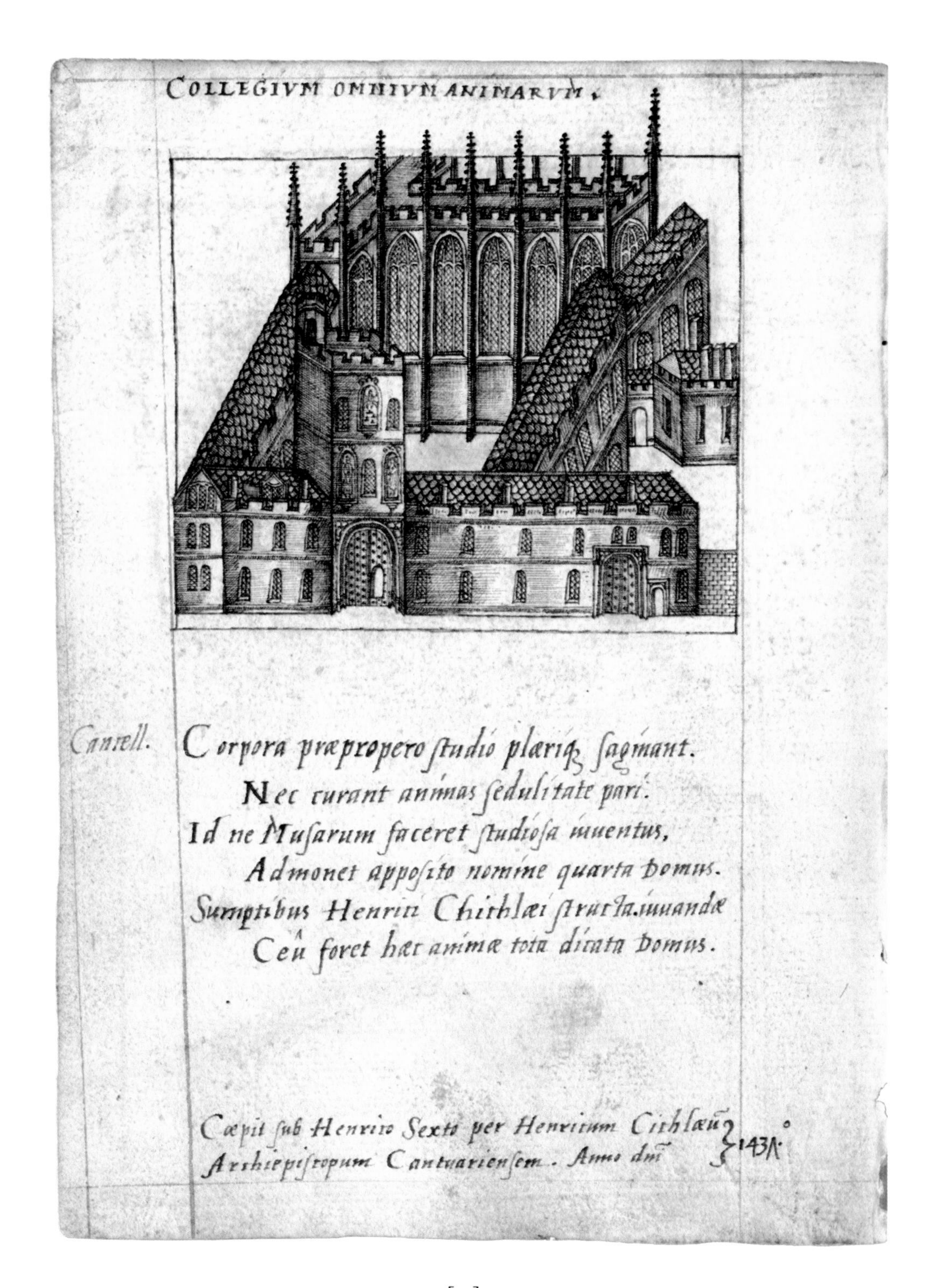

COLLEGIVM OMNIVM ANIMARVM.

Cantrell. Corpora præpropero studio pleriq; saginant.
Nec curant animas sedulitate pari.
Id ne Musarum faceret studiosa iuventus,
Admonet apposito nomine quarta Domus.
Sumptibus Henrici Chichlæi structa iuvandæ
Ceu foret hæc animæ tota dicata Domus.

Cœpit sub Henrico Sexto per Henricum Cichlæum Archiepiscopum Cantuariensem. Anno dni 1437°.

[9v]

Collegium Reginale.

Huic itidem similis Pastor Robertus Eglissfild
Reginæ munus donat & ipse suæ.
Nam Reginalem cum magnis sumptibus ædem
Fundassat, vocat hanc (clara Philippa) tuam.
Fœmina quô musis nutrix, non dura nouerca,
Pergeret, & studijs Mater adesse pia.

Cæpit sub Edowardo tertio per Dnm Robertum Eglyssfild. Sacellanum Dnæ Philippæ. Vxoris eiusdē Edowardi. Anno domini 1340.

[10r]

Collegium Universitatis.

En tibi iam prodit speciosa academia, quæ quum
Sit species, generis nomen adaucta tenet.
Ut logice species generatim sæpe vocatur,
Et pars pro toto corpore sæpe venit.
Huic Dunelmensis Guilielmus præsbyter ædi,
Communi studiis nomen ab urbe, dedit.

Cœpit sub Aluredo, per Dnm Guilielmum Archidiaconum Dunelmensem. Anno dni. 873.

11

Regina interloquitur.

Regina	Illud in his summa puto dignum laude, quod ipsi Noluerint titulis luxuriare suis.
Cancel.	Omnibus hæc eadem laus est communis, habetq; In reliquis itidem laus ea vera locum.
Regina	Summæ laudis erat, gestis tot rebus honestis, Laudibus authores abstinuisse suis.
Cancel.	Tres aliæ restant inclusæ mœnibus ædes. Quas nullo fas est præteriisse modo.

COLLEGIVM ÆNEI NASI.

Æneus hic nasus prælucet. ut insula ponto
Prominet, aut reliquo nasus in ore nitet.
Quæ domus impensis Gulielmi structa Smythæi,
Æneo & æterno nomine digna manet.
Multis illa quidem turbis conferta studentum.
Spes vt sit messis magna futura bonæ.

Cœpit sub Henrico 7° per Gulielmū Smythe episcopū Lincolniensem. Anno dni. } 1513°

10

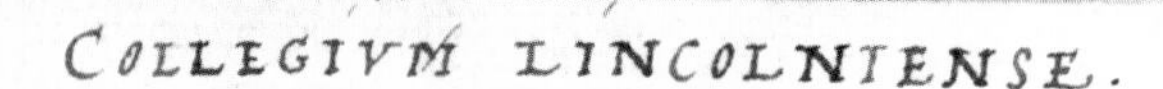
COLLEGIVM LINCOLNIENSE.

Huic latus occiduum claudit Lincolnia sedes.
Quæ sibi Patronos gaudet habere duos.
Alter erat Thomas Rotheram, Richardus & alter
Flemmge, eiusdem Præsul vterq; loci.
Quos vbi ditarat Lincolnia, gratus vterq;,
Non sibi, sed sedi dona dat ista suæ.

Cœpit sub Henrico. 5.° per Richardū Flemmge. episcopū Lincolniensem. Anno Domini. } 1420.°
Auctū per Thomā Rotheram, episcopū lincolniēsem A.° } 1419.°

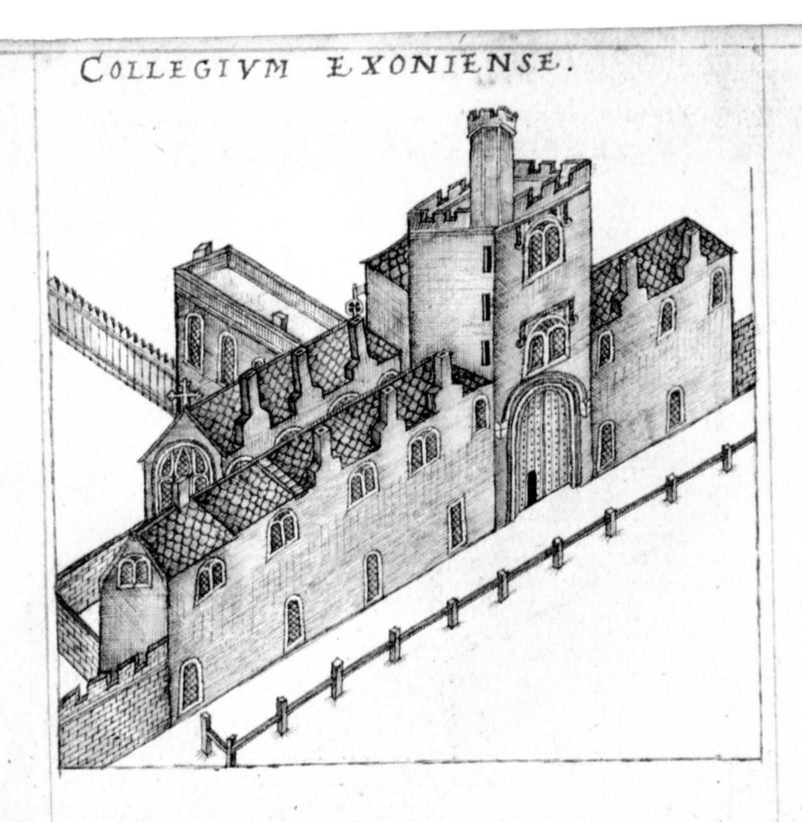

Distat ab Oxonio spatijs Exonia multis,
Et procul occidui vergit ad ora maris.
Attamen Oxonij sedes Exonia fixas
Inuenit, et musis iam fit amica quies.
Condidit has Præsul Gualterus Stapleton ædes.
Indidit et sedi nomina digna suæ.

Cœpit sub Edouardo 2°. per Gualteru͂ Stapleton Episcopum Exoniensem Anno dm͂ } 1316°

Auctu͂ sub Elisabetha Regina, per dnm Guilielmu͂ Petræum ordinis equestris militem inauratum } 1566°

[12v]

13.

Regina interloquitur.

Regina Ô pia pontificum mens hæc: ô tempora fausta,
Quæ tantos clëro progenuere viros.

Cancell. Clërica sit olim concors concordia clëro
Certatim voluit ferre libenter opem.
Sed ne sola suos videatur clërica turba,
Et musas opera velle fouere sua,
Arctica si lubeat pomœria pulchra videre,
Hic parem laicos ferre videbis opem.

Regina Siccine communitis certatũ est viribus, vrbs hæc
Vt fieret studijs tota dicata sacris?
Quin age dic laico quot habemus in ordine, Musas
Auctas hîc opera qui voluere sua.

Cancell. Illud ego (Princeps ter magna) lubentiùs addam,
Tota quòd hîc nostræ laudis harena patet.
Sed mihi restat adhuc prædictis ædibus, intra
Muros, appendix adjicienda priùs.
Quæ tua cum laus sit, (Guilielme Petræe,) lubenter
Reginæ dabis hîc nonnihil vltrò tuæ.
Quòd te præcipuè videatur amare, suisq;
Consilijs præstò semper adesse velit.

Patria te iactat genuisse Devonia, & Vrbs hæc
Gaudet se studijs instituisse suis.
Sumptibus ergò tuis tu gratus vtriq; parenti,
Auxiliatrices reddis vtramq; manus.
Vt quas exiles prius hic Exonia habebat,
Has habeat plenas iam satis aucta domos.
Aucta quidem numero, sed & amplis censibus aucta.
Clara sub imperijs Elisabetha tuis.
Quæ, quales, quantosq; tibi promittat alumnos,
Ex vno disci cætera turba potest.
Is Berblokus erit. tuus dexterrima dextra
Has formas mira dexteritate dedit.
Quin age, macte tua virtute (Petræe) fouendis
Fœtibus hisce tuis quam potes adfer opem.

COLLEGIVM TRINITATIS.

14

Vrbis at egressæ iam mœnia, proxima sedes
Occurrit Thomæ sumptibus aucta Popi.
Quam sacrosanctæ triadis cognomen habere
Iussit inauratus Miles, equestre decus.
Huius adhuc teneros fœtus, pia mater adauget
Coniunx, tam digno coniuge digna suo.

Cœpit sub Maria Regina per Dnm Thomā Popum ordinis equestris militem inauratum. Anno dni. 1556.

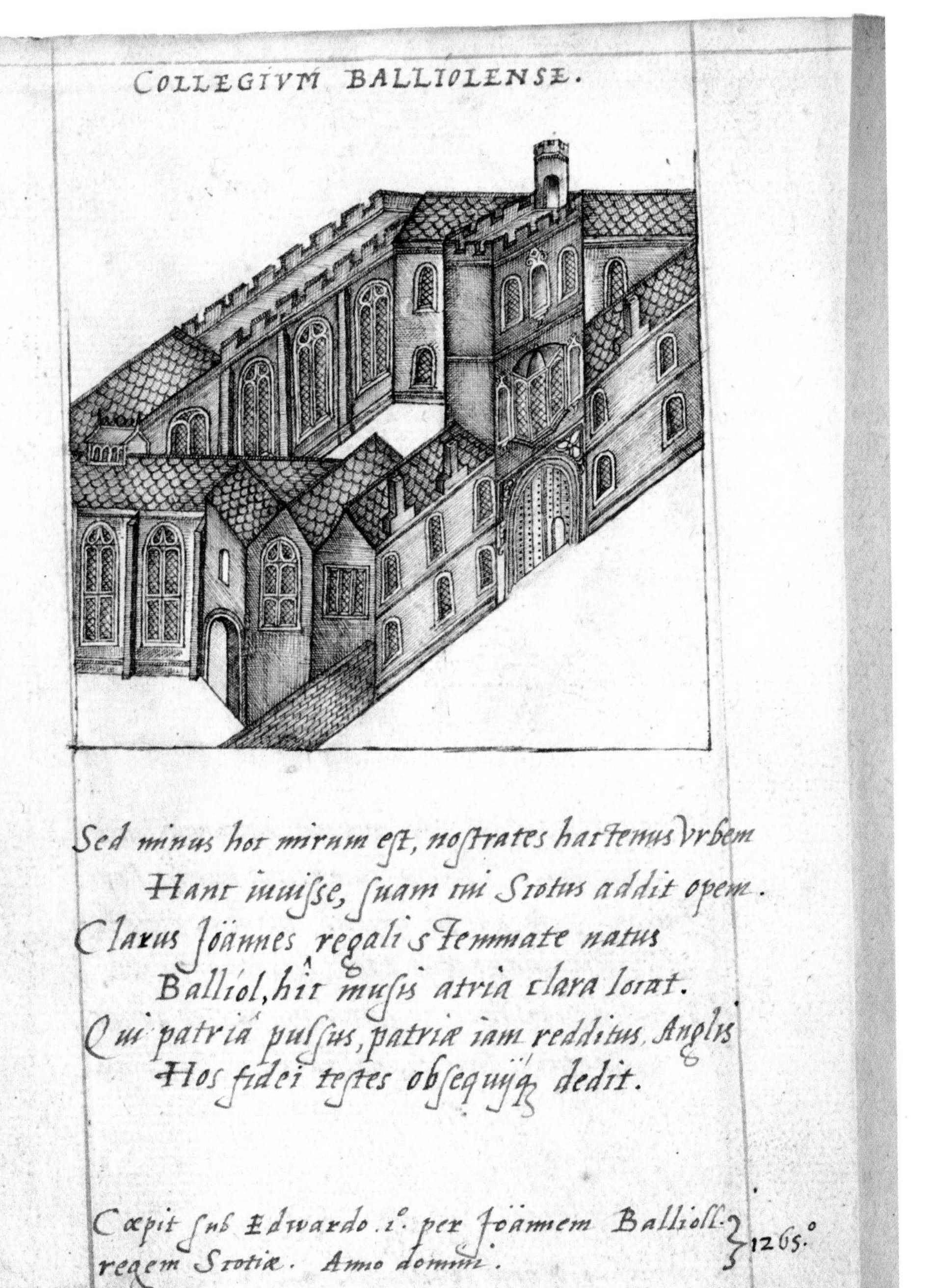

COLLEGIVM BALLIOLENSE.

Sed minus hoc mirum est, nostrates hactenus Vrbem
Hanc inuisse, suam cui Scotus addit opem.
Clarus Ioännes regali stemmate natus
Balliol, hic musis atria clara locat.
Qui patriâ pulsus, patriæ iam redditus, Anglis
Hos fidei testes obsequijq; dedit.

Cœpit sub Edwardo .1°. per Ioānem Balliol-
regem Scotiæ. Anno domini. } 1265°

Transitio ad descriptionem Vltimi Collegij.

15

Vltima postremo iam commemoranda triumpho,
Restat Ioanni sacra dicata domus.
Quæ licet extremo claudatur fine laborum.
Chara vel in primis est tamen illa mihi.
Sicut Iacobo patriarchæ Beniamin olim
(Excepto Ioseph) primus amore fuit.

COLLEGIVM IOANNIS BAPTISTÆ.

Cantell. Has Thomas Whitus, Londini gloria, raras
Mercator merces donat, emitq; suis.
Qui Londinensi bis Prætor in urbe, superstes
Vivit adhuc, equitum non mediocre decus.
Faxit ut ille diu vivat, valeatq; superstes
Musis, at demum cœlica regna petat.

Cœpit sub Maria Regina per Dnm Thomā White, ordinis equestris militem mauratū. Aº dni. 1555

[15v]

16

Cantell. Quod si plura libet paucis audire, superstes
Restat adhuc sacris satra dicata scholis.

Regina Cum age satra mihi schola summe audita placebit.
Et reliquis colophon aedibus aptus erit.

SCHOLA THEOLOGICA.

Caniell. Eminet, & mediæ fastigia suspicit Vrbis,
Dux Humfrede, tuis sumptibus ista schola.
Surgit in immensum turritis vndiq; pinnis.
Sectaq; perpulchro marmore, quadra domus.
Splendida luminibus crebris laquearia fulgent,
Artificumq; nitent pendula saxa manu.

Cœpit sub Henrico .6o. per dominū Humfredum
Ducem Glocestriæ. Anno domini. } 1441.

[16v]

17

SCHOLÆ PVBLICÆ.

Imminet huic series bis quinq; instructa domorũ.
Semita quà studijs omnibus vna patet.
Sumptus hos fecit Regina Maria, deditq;
Vnde nouas possis hasce videre scholas.
Elisabetha soror tu digna sorore Maria,
Pro pietate tua, quas dedit illa, foues.
Gratia ut æqualis iam detur vtriq; sorori.
Altra quôd has foueat, quôd dedit altra scholas.

Transitio ad Aulas, seû hospitia litteraria.

Cancel. His sed adhuc arctis nolens contenta videri
Finibus, est alÿs vrbs quoque culta locis.
Scilicet hæc aulis olim plenissima, Musis
Parturÿt fœtus vrbs populosa nouos.
Quæ noua progenies vrbisque Colonia ducta,
Creuit in immensum viribus aucta suis.
Tempus edax rerum multas absumpsit, & aulæ
Quædam dant dictis ædibus apta loca.
Aulas iam tot habet, quot habent sua nomina Musæ,
Et par est numero turba nouena nouem.

Regina Cum age ne pigeat, cum sis Præfectus & aulis,
Aularum nobis nomina trita dare.

Descriptio Aulæ cerumæ.

Cancel. Harum quæ forma est pulcherrima, proxima tertis
Aula, Wykâme, tuis ordine prima subit.
Quæ licet hîc primas videatur habere, sororum
At nulli laudem detrahit illa suam.
Inclÿta nobilium numerosâ pube referta.
Ceruma â cerui nomine dicta domus.

10

Eminet hæc alijs formæq; situsq; nitore.
Vt cursu canibus cerua præire solet.
Vnde suo merito Cervina hæc dicitur aula.
In media Cerui cornua fronte gerens.

Epitome aliarum Aularum.

In reliquis sermo fiet contractior, octo
Quæ restant varijs vndiq; sparsa locis.
Aulica duntaxat vulgataq; nomina paucis
Attingam, & breuibus puncta notabo metris.

Regina Sed caue, ne nimium dum tu breuis esse laboras,
Obscurus fias hac breuitate tua.

Cancell. Candida, Lata, Noua, studijs ciuilibus apta,
Porta patet Musis, Justiniane, tuis.
Quæ restant, alijs discendis artibus aulæ,
Sunt propriæ, quibus hæc nomina prisca manet.
Sacra Mariæ, Alburnensis, Glocestria, diui
Edmundi, at demum Magdalis aula frequens.

Peroratio Cancellarij.

His inclusa modis en qualiacunq; ducatus
Septa mei, Princeps Elisabetha, vides.

Regina Ex his iam tandem, Roberte, intelligo, cur tu
Dux magis hîc, alibi quâm Comes esse velis.

Næ tu præclarum nactus videare Ducatum.
Cui sunt tantorũ tot monumenta virûm.
Siccine currenti (quod vulgo dicitur) istis
Carminibus properas subdere calcar equo.
Vt magis hæc lubeat præsentia cernere, quæ tu
Magnifico narras ore stupenda loca.
Cancell. Quód si audita placent, multo magis ista placebũt,
Si præsens oculis hauseris ista tuis.
Regina Cum age tu comitem mihi te (Comes inclyte) præbe.
Vt monstres digitis quæ modó lingua docet.
Cancell. Hoc equidem faciam promptus, gratesq; laboris
Huius suscepti nomine gratus agam.
Cum & tota cohors mecum prostrata studẽtum
Aduoluet genibus se resupina tuis.
Quæ cum multa tibi (Princeps preclara) tuisq;
Debeat, hoc vno nomine tota tua est.
Quód Musis olim Mæcenas alter adesse,
Cum pater Henricus cœperit ille tuus,
Et dederit studijs stipendia digna fouendis,
Publica lectorum uox quibus ore præit,
Tu proles tali tantoq; simillima Patri
Hæc larga foueas continuata manu.

19

Dum quas radices pater hic plantauit, easdem
Æmula munifico filia rore rigas.
Sic sic perge tuo non impar esse parenti,
Patrizans Patri ~~patri~~ par pietate pari.
Nec dubita quicquam, quin incrementa daturus
Sit Deus, & sumptu præmia digna tuo.
Interea vero communi nomine grates,
Quas summas habet, vrbs hæc tibi tota refert.
Priuatimq; sacræ linguæ prælector hebræus
Priuato grates nomine gratus agit.
Qui tibi ne sterilis maneat, vel inutilis arbor
fructus, quos potuit plantula ferre, tulit.
Tu quales quales fructus (clarissima Princeps)
Oblatos hilari fronte, manuq; lege.

Gratulatio hebraica in aduentum eiusdem
Principis illustriss.ae Dnæ Elisabethæ
ab eodem hebraice conscripta.

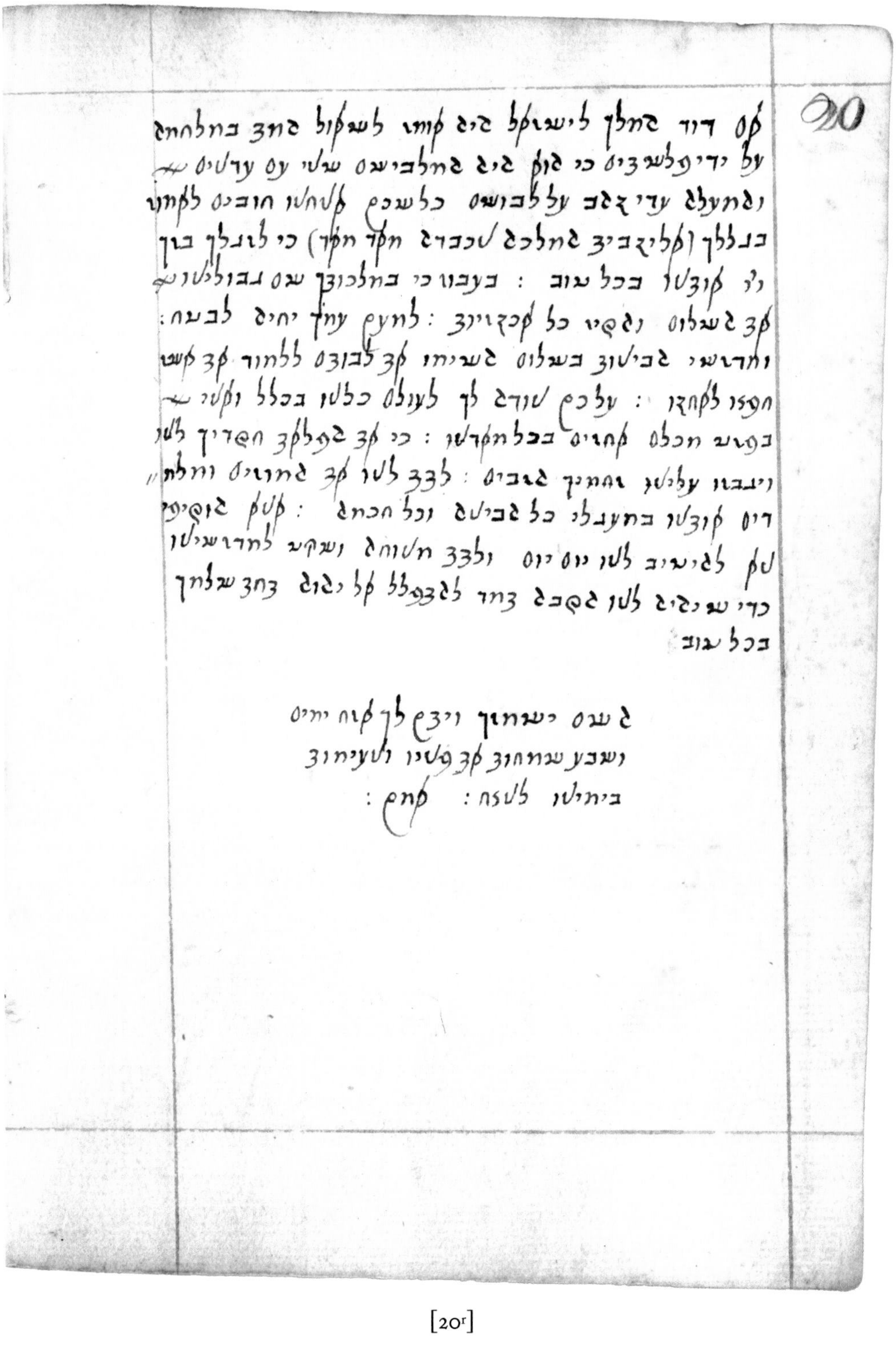

20

אם דוד המלך לישראל היה אומר לשאול המת במלחמה
על ידי פלשתים כי הוא היה המלבישם שני עם עדנים
והמעלה עדי זהב על לבושם כלשכם אנחנו חובים לקונן
בגללך (אליזבית המלכה לכבודה אקר אקר) כי לנגלך ברך
י״י אותנו בכל טוב : בעבור כי במלכותך שם גבולינו
את השלום ונהפו כל אכזריות : למען עמך יחיה לבטח :
ומדרשי הבינות בשלום השירו את לבותם ללמוד את קשת
חפצו לקחתו : על כן טורה לך לעולם כלנו בכלל וקטן
בפרט מכלם אחרים בבלמדרשו : כי את האלקת חסדיך לנו
ויגברו עלינו ותמיך גברים : לתת לנו את האורים ותלמי״
דים אותנו במעגלי כל הבינה וכל חכמה : אמן הופיעי
עם לגיטיב לנו יום יום ולתת מנוחה ושקט למדרשינו
כדי שנהיה לנו הפבה תמיד לתפלל אל יהוה תחת שלטונך
בכל טוב

השם ישמרך ויתן לך אורח ימים
ושבע שמחות את פניך ונעימות
בימינך לנצח : אמן :

21

אשירה הרעי כלנו יחדיו ונעלזו :

גילי מאד אכספורד קרית ספר :
הריעי טובה הנה מקור כלשכל :
הנה אליזביט המלכה באה לך :
והשרה אדונה משכנת בך :

ברוך יי אלהים ברום :
מביאך הנה בשלום :
ומקוה אותך עד הלום :
ישמרו חייך בכל מקום :

יתן יי לך כלבבך :
וימלא את כל עצתך :
ישמרו את בואך וצאתך :
מכל פגע רע לא יפגשך :

יצליח כל משלח ידך :
אשר נתן אל לבבך :
לא יאונה רע עליך :
לא יקרב באהלך :

תחיה את אליזביט המלכה :
ותהיה מאד מאד הדורה :
ירבה ימיה אל הכבודה :
ויחייה יי בשלום אותה :
אמן ואמן :

תומס נילוש :

4. TRANSLATIONS

i. The Topographical Delineation of the Colleges and Public Schools of the University of Oxford

Translated from the Latin by Sarah Knight

[ii^{v}] THE IMAGE OF HEBREW LEARNING

Do you see how this tree flourishes when its roots are secure?
How it is enriched by its leaves spreading here and there?
The tree is an image of Hebrew learning, which rejoices to have
had its leaves enriched
By your financial generosity, Elizabeth.
God as sower first planted this tree in Paradise.
He ordered mortals to speak Hebrew words.
Once upon a time your distinguished father brought this here,
You, devout Elizabeth, water the roots.
And so the tree brings forth this fruit appropriate to you,
Cultivated (O greatest of Princes) by what you have spent.

[iv^{r}] DEDICATORY EPISTLE

To the most serene and most venerable Princess, Lady Elizabeth, Queen of England, France and Scotland, defender of the Christian faith etc., let all things be auspicious and fortunate.

Behold (most distinguished Princess Elizabeth), you hold a certain topographical delineation of the Colleges and public schools of your University of Oxford, partly represented by draughtsman's pen, partly in poetic verse in the form of a Dialogue, so that you might have the University's entire likeness to hand, as if laid out before your eyes for your consideration. The University's inhabitants devote themselves to all liberal arts under this most auspicious reign of yours, just as if they were safe under the shield of Minerva, and they strive no more passionately and steadfastly on behalf of best and greatest God, than all of them strive to be able to offer their diligence, trust and hard work to you, as much as they owe, in all earnest. At any rate, although the method of delineating this University might be through a duller and less polished art, in terms both of the drawing and the verse, yet it could still be seen as worthy of your royal Majesty's sight, and you will have mercy (or so I hope) on these first attempts at a new undertaking. These attempts were made with no other intention than to welcome your most serene Majesty on this most ardently desired visit to us. I would like to ask your royal Majesty – most humbly, as a suppliant – for your opinion whether in general

[iv[v]]

it could happen (most distinguished Princess) that, just as
For painters and poets
There should always be an equal opportunity to venture whatever
they like,
so you by no means would wish me to be prevented from that; for in the meantime, while I attribute part of the dialogue to an interlocutor with the most eminent name of your royal Majesty, I in turn adapt the other part to Lord Robert Dudley, Earl of Leicester, our most worthy Chancellor. Observe both sides as I (or so I hope) honour both your person and his. Next, the Dialogue's argument is fashioned in such a way that it can seem to have been chosen from a separate moment, or from the present circumstances, exactly as if the Chancellor had asked you (most noble Queen), as you were about to depart from Woodstock, when at last it pleased you to set out, whether he could seize the opportunity to lay out the path of the future topographical narrative before you, as it were. If this work, of whatever kind it may be, could only be pleasing to your Royal pre-eminence alone, then it would be both more pleasing to others and most pleasing of all to me. May best and greatest God ensure that you thrive for as long as possible.

Her most dutiful pupil, Thomas Neale, Oxford Professor of Hebrew, to her most Serene Majesty.

[3v] (DIALOGUE BETWEEN QUEEN ELIZABETH AND THE EARL OF LEICESTER)

A dialogue of welcome for the coming of the most serene Queen, Lady ELIZABETH, between the aforementioned Queen and Lord Robert Dudley, Earl of Leicester and Chancellor of the University of Oxford.

[4r] THE QUEEN AND THE CHANCELLOR OF OXFORD CONVERSE

Chancellor:
Elizabeth, dear to your subjects and pillar of the British kingdom,
Are you going to leave your home?

Queen:
I am not going to leave for abroad, to travel far as a foreigner,
But where I am going, that entire city is my home.

Chancellor:
What are you describing, thrice-great Prince,
For the entire site of the kingdom is your home.

Queen:
And so, since I have many homes, and many houses,
Why should I not frequently change my house?

Chancellor:
But if, by your leave, I might be allowed to know, I would gladly
Know where your journey is tending.

Queen:
I am going towards Oxford, I seek the house
Dedicated to the Muses, accompanied by my own Muses.

Chancellor:
And why has so great a reason come up for seeing the Muses there,
Since there is a retinue of Muses present at home?

Queen:
That very retinue of Muses present at home
Urged me to visit these sacred houses.

[4^{v}]

Chancellor:
Indeed you pay deserved rewards to your own Muses,
While you prepare to see places sacred to the Muses.

Queen
In all honesty, will I see anything new?
Is there anything worthy of a Prince's visit?

Chancellor:
An ancient city which must be seen will lie open before your eyes,
And the citizens will faithfully kiss your hands.

Queen:
Yet what will I see besides that is worthy or memorable?
What reward will be worth such great effort?

Chancellor:
Most importantly, you will see the houses of fifteen Muses,
A city for which there is no equal throughout Europe.

Queen:
So do you know these houses, then, which the Thames, that
Famous river, surrounds on both sides with its stream?

Chancellor:
Why should I not know? For a long time I have willingly undertaken
To be their leader, nor do I dislike being leader.

Queen:
If all at once you wanted to be Leader of the Muses,
Who would you say should be Earl of Leicester?

[5r]

Chancellor:
It is no less to have a reputation for learning than for military might,
Both the name of Leader and that of Earl gives me pleasure.

Queen:
But briefly explain to me the names of these houses,
Who, for whom, what patron and creator carried out the work.

Chancellor:
I will indeed do that, with as much brevity as will let me
Recount a few appropriate details in a few more verses.

[5v] CHRIST CHURCH

First stands the large House of the south, Christ Church,
Already worthy of first place because of the two parts of its name;
Then both because it has you and your father, as patron,
And because that group of inhabitants is bigger than the rest.
It was established at Thomas Wolsey's expense,
But increased thanks to the wealth of Henry your father.

Established under Henry VIII, by the help of Thomas Wolsey,
Archbishop of York, in the year of Our Lord 1529.
Finished under the same Henry VIII, in the year of Our Lord 1546.

[6r] THE QUEEN SPEAKS

Queen:
And so might it happen that, since that house can support many,
When it is full it might not completely support its own members?

Chancellor:
That house supports as many as is thought right to be nurtured,
And would nurture more if it grew as a result of the acquisition of more property.
But the untimely death of your father, a death hated by the Muses,
Meant that this could be the place for more.

Queen:
And so it is up to the person who can to be helpful: a suitable shape
Is given more quickly to prepared material.

[6v] ORIEL COLLEGE

Chancellor:
But I'll move on to the rest. Oriel stands as the seventh home
Of the Muses, O, truly it is called a royal house.
Venerable in age, those times of Edward witnessed it,
The king who was the second of that name.
A certain Adam with the surname Browne built it,
And he took its name from his king.

Established under Edward II by Master Adam Browne. Almoner of the same Edward, in the year of Our Lord 1323.

[7r] CORPUS CHRISTI COLLEGE

The fifth bids us to be mindful of our salvation,
Teaching us how and whence that salvation is generated.
When his body was taken into heaven, Christ the Lord gave us salvation,
It takes its name from the name of Christ's body.
Richard Foxe supported this college lavishly with great riches,
And created a place suitable for the Muses.

Established under Henry VII by Richard Foxe, Bishop of Winchester,
in the year of Our Lord 1516.

[7v] MERTON COLLEGE

Not far from there stands Merton, which is the sixth in order,
Called in full the House of Merton.
Walter Merton was the President (under whose bishopric Rochester
Flourished), he was patron and creator of this House.
Although this dutiful mother has nurtured many pupils,
The sacred house would yet be suitable for more.

Established under Edward I by Walter Merton Bishop of Rochester,
in the year of Our Lord 1276.

[8r] NEW COLLEGE

The next to follow is full enough and packed with a crowd
Of students, which for a long time has acquired the name of a new group.
This college shines throughout the sky with its high towers, laden
With the rare jewels of learning for those who live within.
Bishop William Wykeham founded this place, offspring born under
A thrice blessed star in Wykeham's city.

Established under Richard II by William of Wykeham, Bishop of Winchester,
in the year of Our Lord 1375.

[8v] MAGDALEN COLLEGE

Nor is the house dedicated to Mary less full of renown,
Whose faith the religious cohorts of Magdalen teach;
The shining roofs bear witness to its generous patron,
A worthy rival in splendour, Wykeham, for you.
William Waynflete named this place, himself a unique pupil
And one of your flock, great Wykeham.

Established under Henry VI by William Waynflete, Bishop of Winchester, in the year of Our Lord 1459.

[9r] THE CHANCELLOR SPEAKS

Chancellor:
The rest of the Colleges should be described in similar words,
If the length of time taken would not bore you.

Queen:
Go on: recount the names *first* given to the rest,
These will prompt no boredom in my ears.

[9v] ALL SOULS COLLEGE

Chancellor:
I will skip quickly over bodies, which most people passionately
indulge,
But they do not look after their souls with similar care:
So that young men passionate about the Muses do not do this,
The fourth house reminds them, with its suitable name.
Built by the wealth of Henry Chichele, this entire House
Would be dedicated to helping the soul.

Established under Henry VI by Henry Chichele, Archbishop of Canterbury, in the year of Our Lord 1437.

[10r] THE QUEEN'S COLLEGE

Similarly, the priest Robert Eglesfield himself gave a gift to his Queen.
For when he had established the Queen's house with copious wealth,
He named this after you (distinguished Philippa):
A woman who would act as a nurse to the Muses, not as a harsh
step-mother,
And would be a holy Mother to learning.

Established under Edward III by Master Robert Eglesfield. The chaplain of Lady Philippa, wife of the same Edward, in the year of Our Lord 1340.

[10v] UNIVERSITY COLLEGE

Behold, now a handsome college comes into view, which whatever
Its form might be has increased the reputation of its type,
Just as in logic the form is often named according to types,
And the part often stands in for the whole.
To this foundation William priest of Durham gave the name
Derived from a city collectively given over to learning.

Established under Alfred, by Master William, Archdeacon of Durham, in the year of Our Lord 873.

[11r] THE QUEEN SPEAKS

Queen:
I think these men worthy of the highest praise because they themselves
Did not want to glory in their own titles.

Chancellor:
This same praise is shared by all, and that genuine praise should similarly be applied to the rest.

Queen:
It was worthy of the highest praise, that when they had performed so many honourable deeds,
The founders refrained from praising themselves.

Chancellor:
Three other foundations remain, enclosed within the walls,
Which it is in no way right to neglect.

[11v] BRASENOSE COLLEGE

A nose of bronze gleams upon this, as an island stands out in the sea,
Or a nose shines out from the rest of the face.
This house, built at the expense of William Smith,
Remains worthy of an eternal name set in bronze.
Indeed it is packed with many crowds of students,
So that there is great hope for a good harvest in the future.

Established under Henry VII by William Smith, Bishop of Lincoln, in the year of Our Lord 1513.

[12r] LINCOLN COLLEGE

The foundation of Lincoln surrounds the western side of this place,
Which delights in possessing two patrons.
One was Thomas Rotheram, and the other Richard Fleming,
Both president of the same place.
When Lincoln had enriched them, each one was pleased
To give that gift not to himself, but to his foundation.

Established under Henry V by Richard Fleming, Bishop of Lincoln,
in the year of Our Lord 1420.
Augmented by Thomas Rotheram, Bishop of Lincoln,
in the year of Our Lord 1479.

[12v] EXETER COLLEGE

Exeter is at a great distance from Oxford,
And lies far away on the coast of the western sea.
Nevertheless Exeter has found secure dwelling in Oxford,
And has now brought companionable tranquility to the Muses.
Walter Stapleton, the President, built this foundation,
And gave it a name worthy of his seat.

Established under Edward II by Walter Stapleton, Bishop of Exeter,
in the year of Our Lord 1316. Augmented under Queen Elizabeth by
Master William Petre, Knight, 1566.

[13r] THE QUEEN SPEAKS

Queen:
O, how devout are the minds of prelates? O, blessed age,
Which produced such great men from the clergy.

Chancellor:
Once upon a time harmonious clerical union
Freely and willingly wanted to help the clergyman thus.
But so that the group of clergymen do not just seem to
Want to support their own people and Muses through their work,
If it would please you to see the beautiful spaces near the city
boundaries to the north,
You will see that these men brought equal help to the laity.

Queen:
And so did they join forces and strive so that this city
Might become entirely dedicated to sacred learning?
Go on, tell me how many we possess in the rank of the laity,
Who wished to increase the Muses through their own efforts here.

Chancellor:
Thrice-great Prince, I will gladly mention that,
Because here the whole arena for our praise should lie open.
But it still remains for me to add first as an appendix the colleges
within
The walls, of which I spoke earlier,
Since this praise should be yours, (William Petre), you will gladly
Give something to your queen here of your own accord,
Since he seems to love you above all,
And always wants to be on hand with his advice.

[13v]

Devon your homeland boasts to have produced you, and this city
Rejoices to have educated you with its learning.
And so you should be thankful for your wealth from both parents,
And you should give helping hands to both.
Just as this Exeter formerly had exiles here,
Now, increased sufficiently in size, let these houses be full.
Increased indeed in number, but also increased in abundance of wealth.
Distinguished under your reign, Elizabeth.
What kind of students, and how great the students are that this place produces for you,
The rest of the crowd can learn from this one individual.
That man will be Bereblock, whose most dexterous right hand
Created these images with marvellous dexterity.
And so go forth, glorify in your virtue, Petre, and help these
Offspring of yours who must be nurtured, as much as you can.

[14r] TRINITY COLLEGE

But now, having ventured outside the city walls, we have come to
The next foundation, increased by the wealth of Thomas Pope.
The gilded soldier, ornament of knighthood, ordered
That it should have the name of the Holy Trinity.
The holy mother increased the offspring of this college, who are still young,
A spouse so worthy of her worthy spouse.

Established under Queen Mary under Master Thomas Pope, Knight,
in the year of Our Lord 1556.

[14v] BALLIOL COLLEGE

But it is less amazing that so far natives have helped this city,
To which a Scotsman adds his assistance.
Distinguished John Balliol, born from royal stock,
Provided distinguished homes for the Muses here.
Driven from his homeland, now returned to his homeland,
He gave the English these testaments of his good faith and allegiance.

Established under Edward I by John Balliol, king of Scotland,
in the year of Our Lord 1265.

[15r] TRANSITION TO THE DESCRIPTION OF THE LAST COLLEGE

Finally, the last now to be mentioned in triumph,
The holy house dedicated to John remains,
Which allows the last purpose of our labours to be completed.
That house is especially dear to me,
Just as Benjamin was once the most beloved,
(With the exception of Joseph), to Jacob his father.

[15v] THE COLLEGE OF JOHN THE BAPTIST

Chancellor:
Thomas White, the glory of London, merchant,
Gave this rare wealth to the college, and bought it with his own.
He was twice Lord Mayor of the city of London, survives
And lives still, by no means a mediocre ornament to the knightly rank.
He made sure that he would live for a long time, and that he
would survive
and flourish for the Muses, until at last he seeks the heavenly kingdom.

Established under Queen Mary by Master Thomas White, Knight,
in the year of Our Lord 1557.

[16^{r}]

Chancellor:
If it would please you to hear more in a few words, the sacred school
remains yet, dedicated to the sacred.

Queen:
Go on, it will give me the greatest pleasure to hear about the sacred school,
And it shall be a suitable postscript to the rest of the foundations.

[16^{v}] DIVINITY SCHOOL

Chancellor:
That school built at your expense is conspicuous, and pushes out its
Heights in the middle of the city, Duke Humfrey.
It rises up into boundless dimensions, with its distinguished towers,
Divided by beautiful marble, a four-cornered house.
Its radiant panelled ceilings glow, due to abundant candlelight,
And the stones hanging down gleam, through the hand of the craftsmen.

Established under Henry VI by Master Humfrey Duke of Gloucester. In the year of Our Lord 1447.

[17^{r}] PUBLIC SCHOOLS

From this place a double row of buildings is laid out,
A path that opens the way to all forms of learning.
Queen Mary was responsible for the expense, which she donated,
And so you can witness these new schools.
Elizabeth, a sister worthy of your sister Mary,
On account of your devotion, you nurture those schools she donated.
May equal thanks now be given to either sister,
For one nurtures these schools which the other donated.

[17v] TRANSITION TO THE HALLS, OR THE LODGING-PLACES OF LEARNING

Chancellor:
But the city does not wish to rest content at these northern
Boundaries, for it is cultured in other places.
In former times, when it was packed with halls, this densely
  peopled city
Produced new offspring for the Muses.
The new breed, extending the province of the city,
Grew into boundless numbers, increased by their own strength.
Time, the devourer of all things, took many of them away,
And some halls provided suitable places for dedicated foundations.
Now there are as many halls as the Muses have names,
And their ninefold group has the same number, nine.

Queen:
Go on, it will not be burdensome, since you are also in charge of the halls,
To tell me the familiar names of the halls.

DESCRIPTION OF HART HALL

Chancellor:
The most beautiful of these in appearance is the hall that comes
First in sequence next to your house, Wykeham.
Although the latter seems to possess the foremost of the Muses,
Yet the former is in no respect without its own praise.
Famous and packed with the numerous offspring of the nobility,
Hart Hall, so called after the name of the hart.

[18r]

This stands out from the others in appearance and in splendour of
location.
Just as the hart is used to outrunning dogs in its course.
Consequently this hall is named after the Hart on its own merits,
Bearing the horns of the hart in the middle of its exterior.

SYNOPSIS OF THE OTHER HALLS

As for the rest, my speech will be shorter: there are eight
Which remain, scattered throughout in different places.
I shall touch in only a few words on the halls and their well-known
names, and I will mention pertinent facts in short verses.

Queen:
But beware, in case, while trying too hard to be brief,
You become incomprehensible due to this brevity of yours.

Chancellor:
White Hall, Broadgate Hall, New Inn Hall, fit for civil learning,
The gate lies open for your Muses, Justinian.
Those halls that remain to teach other arts
Are special, and still possess these ancient names,
St Mary, St Alban, Gloucester, St
Edmund, and finally the crowded hall of Magdalen.

THE CHANCELLOR'S PERORATION

Contained within these verses, behold, Queen Elizabeth,
You see the place enclosed under my leadership.

Queen:
From this I understand at last, Robert, why you
Want more to be leader here, than to be Earl elsewhere.

[18v]

Certainly you seem to have acquired an outstanding leadership,
Since you preside over so many monuments of such great men.
In fact, are you rushing to spur on a willing horse (as is commonly said)
With those verses of yours,
So that it may be more pleasing to see these marvellous places in actuality,
Which you have recounted with a mouth full of praise?

Chancellor:
If what you have heard has pleased you, it will please you much more
If you drink them in with your eyes in person.

Queen:
Go on, prove yourself a companion to me (distinguished Earl),
And point out with your fingers what you have only recited with your tongue.

Chancellor:
I shall do that promptly, and, thankful, I give you thanks
In the name of this task I have undertaken.
Indeed, the whole group of students along with me prostrates itself,
And throws itself forward at your knees.
For this group (distinguished Queen) owes much to you and yours,
And all of it is yours under this one name.
Once a second Maecenas appeared for the Muses,
When that father of yours, Henry, established
And bestowed stipends worthy of supporting learning,
The public voice of Readers whose mouths resounded:
You, his descendant, most similar to your father in quality and greatness,
Should continue to support these, with generous hand.

[19r]

While your father planted roots here,
As his daughter you should strive to moisten those same roots with abundant watering.
Continue thus, do not be unequal to your father,
Taking after your father, equal your father's equal devotion.
Do not doubt that God will grant increase, and rewards worthy of your donation.
Meanwhile, this entire city gives thanks to you under its shared name,
For it possesses the greatest thanks.
Privately the Hebrew Praelector of the sacred language,
Thankful, gives thanks to you under his own name.
He hopes that this should not be barren to you, or that a useless tree
Bore fruit, which a little plant might bear.
You, most eminent Queen, read such fruit as is offered to you
With a happy expression, and read it in your own hand.

ii. Gratulatory Address and Poem

Translated from the Hebrew by Helen Spurling

[19v]

Hebrew gratulation for the coming of the same most venerable Princess Lady Elizabeth, written by the same man in Hebrew.

[20r]

If David the king of Israel was saying of Saul, the one who died in battle by the hands of the Philistines: 'For he was the one who clothed them in scarlet delicately, the one who put ornaments of gold upon their garment' [i.e. adaption of 2 Samuel 1:24], [then], O every inhabitant, we are [even more] duty-bound to speak on account of you [i.e. Elizabeth]. So let us greatly honour Elizabeth the queen, because for your sake the Lord blessed us with every goodness. For in your kingdom he established our borders with peace and removed all cruelty in order that your people may live in security. And they established their minds in peace with interpretations of understandings to teach the knowledge they are delighted to possess. Therefore, we will praise you forever, all of us in general and I in particular from all of the others, with all our strength. For you, you have done your kindnesses wonderfully for us and your great compassion prevails over us, [particularly] to give to us those who instruct and teach us in the courses of all understanding and all wisdom. Please continue now to show goodness to us daily and to give rest and quietness to our teachings as much as that it may be for us the turn of affairs continually to pray to the Lord under your peace with every goodness.

May The Name [i.e. the Lord] guard you and give you a long life and seven joys in addition to his presence and songs in our days forever. Amen.

[21r]

Let us sing, raise a shout all of us together and let us say:

Rejoice greatly, O Oxford, city of the book
Raise a shout, O great city, fountain of all wisdom
Behold Elizabeth the queen comes to you
And the princess, her majesty is established in you

Blessed is the Lord, Most High on high
He brings you here in peace
And leads you up to here
He guards your life in every place

The Lord gives you according to your desire
And he fulfils too all your plan
He guards your coming-in and your going-out
From every evil contact to your soul

He causes every deed of your hand to prosper
Which you give your heart
Evil will not meet you
It will not approach your tents

May Elizabeth the queen live long
And her majesty be very great indeed
May the Lord increase her glory
And may the Lord cause her to live in peace

Amen and Amen

Thomas Neale

NOTES ON THE DRAWINGS

Louise Durning

The opportunity has been taken here to order the drawings according to the likely original structure of the manuscript, but they are identified by their current folio numbering.

The principal sources for the architectural history of the buildings discussed are: John Newman, 'The Physical Setting', in J. McConica (ed.), *The Collegiate University (The History of the University of Oxford,* vol. iii; Oxford, 1986), 597–633; R. H. C. Davis, 'The Chronology of Perpendicular Architecture in Oxford', *Oxoniensia,* 11–12 (1946–7), 75–89; J. H. Harvey, 'Architecture in Oxford 1350–1500', in J. Catto and J. R. Evans (eds.), *Late Medieval Oxford (History of the University of Oxford,* vol. ii; Oxford, 1992), 747–68; Royal Commission on Historic Monuments, *City of Oxford* (London, 1939); H. E. Salter and M. D. Lobell (eds.), *The University of Oxford (The Victoria History of the County of Oxfordshire,* vol. iii; Oxford, 1954). Additional sources used for the study of individual buildings are indicated at the end of each note.

FOL. ii^{v} – THE IMAGE OF HEBREW LEARNING

For discussion of the meaning of the emblem see introductory essay, pages 30–32. A second version of the emblem also appears as a frontispiece to Thomas Neale's collection of Rabbinic commentaries and translations presented to Queen Elizabeth at the same time as the Topographical Delineation (BL MS. Royal 2 D. xxi, fol. 1).

FOL. 5^{v} – CHRIST CHURCH

The buildings shown were those erected by Thomas Wolsey to house his new foundation, Cardinal College, begun in 1525 and left unfinished by the time of his fall from power in 1529. Refounded as Christ Church by

Henry VIII in 1546. Even in its incomplete state this was by far the most magnificent college in England, built on a palatial scale. Bereblock's choice of viewpoint 'edits out' the unfinished portions of the site, concentrating attention instead on the great hall, with its three-tiered louvre, the domestic range at right angles to it – where the Queen stayed during the visit – and opposite, the completed parts of the gatehouse range, which presented the showpiece front to South Street (now St Aldate's). Within the quadrangle, the fragments of the unfinished cloister, on the ground floor of the hall and lodging range, are indicated. The tall battlemented tower at the angle between these two ranges, which housed the stairs to the hall, was actually continuous with the hall but in the drawing it has been represented diagonally, perhaps to more conveniently display its volume and the panelled stonework of the entrance arch (which can still be seen, though the present upper stages of the tower are nineteenth-century work.). The tower is clearly shown as unroofed, but it would appear to have risen high above the lodging range to the right (note the door opening on to the lead roof). Architectural historians have disagreed over the intended function of this structure and whether it was intended to be a bell tower or a treasury (muniment) tower. Bereblock's suggestion of one large louvred, or grilled, opening, without stone mullions, may suggest that a bell tower is the more likely hypothesis. The dramatic skyline of heraldic carvings and battlements on the street front was replaced in the seventeenth century with a balustraded parapet but the richly modelled polygonal buttresses of the lower stages of the gatehouse are still in place, upon which Tom Tower, designed by Sir Christopher Wren, was raised in 1681–2.

Martin Biddle, 'Wolsey's Bell Tower', *Oxoniensia,* 53 (1988), 205–10; Mavis Batey and Catherine Cole,'The Great Staircase at Christ Church', *Oxoniensia,* 53 (1988), 211–20.

FOL. 8 – NEW COLLEGE

In the proposed reconstruction of the manuscript, this would have formed a double-page spread with the image of Christ Church.

The buildings shown here were completed in about 1404, having been built to a single coherent plan around a large quadrangle. This was the first of the colleges to be so planned and it became an important model for the subsequent development of collegiate planning. Bereblock's view is not so concerned with this quadrangular arrangement. He has selected instead an external view which shows off the spectacular multi-windowed hall and chapel range, with its forest of pinnacles, alluded to in Neale's verse, and its two great towers, the muniment tower adjoining the hall, which acted as a treasury for keeping valuable documents and plate, and the bell tower at the west end of the chapel (whose windows are much exaggerated).

The crenellated wall with projecting bastion forming the base of the drawing is actually part of the city wall, which formed the boundary to this part of the New College site. The tall, narrow-windowed building shown at the back of the site is the Long House, a palatial lavatory block, whose entire lower floor functioned as the cesspit for the privies above.

G. Jackson-Stops, chapters 5 and 6 in J. Buxton and P. Williams (eds.), *New College, Oxford* (Oxford, 1979).

FOL. 8v – MAGDALEN COLLEGE

The college shares many features with the design of New College, where the founder, William Wayneflete, had himself been a fellow. This, and his friendship with New College's founder, are celebrated in the verse. The drawing focuses on the architectural riches of the external courtyard or Base Court of the college complex (now called St John's Quadrangle) lying at right angles to the High Street, and dispenses with the need to show the interior of the main quadrangle which lies beyond. Bereblock shows the three-bayed west end of the chapel with its richly carved door, and its adjoining muniment tower. These two buildings actually lie parallel to each other but in the drawing have been 'splayed' so that each reads as a separate volume, the depth of the tower being greatly exaggerated. The distinctive external pulpit set in the angle to the right of the chapel is also given great emphasis. Behind the muniment tower is the Founder's

Tower, the principal entrance to the cloistered quadrangle within. These buildings were largely complete by 1490, but the lead-roofed range running from the Founder's Tower to the precinct wall is part of the relatively new President's Lodgings, mostly of the 1530s and 1550s–60s (rebuilt in the 1880s). The small building in the foreground outside the precinct wall is the grammar school, built in the early 1480s. It no longer survives.

The profuse display of battlements on the buildings of this college, compared to the others shown by Bereblock, serves as a potent reminder of how uncommon these were in college buildings before the seventeenth century. These were a marker of special dignity and are usually found only in gatehouses or chapels. The battlementing at the Magdalen complex is another signifier of its magnificence.

FOL. 9^v – ALL SOULS COLLEGE

All Souls, established by Henry Chichele, Archbishop of Canterbury in 1437, had a major role as a chantry foundation, to offer masses for the souls of the King, the dead of the recent wars with France, and 'all the faithful departed'. The great T-shaped chapel, built in 1438–42, dominates the drawing. The hall, lying transversely to the east end of the chapel, this has been diminished in height (compare with Loggan's view), and Bereblock, strangely, adds an imaginary east window to the chapel. The upper stages of the gate tower, opening on to the High Street, are skewed to left to allow the display of an uninterrupted run of chapel windows, but careful attention is paid to the sculptures of the Archbishop and King Henry VI flanking the central window and to the upper panel showing Christ in Judgement. In the lower stages of the gate Bereblock has exaggerated the height of the archway, running it up through two floors. The eastward extension from the quadrangle, with its own gateway and small door, was a new Warden's Lodging, completed in 1553.

H. M. Colvin and J. S. G. Simmons, *All Souls: An Oxford College and Its Buildings (The Chichele Lectures: 1986;* Oxford, 1988).

FOL. 7 – CORPUS CHRISTI COLLEGE

In the proposed reconstruction of the manuscript, this would have formed a double-page spread with the image of All Souls.

The building of the quadrangle of Corpus Christi was begun in 1512–13 and completed by about 1517. Once again, Bereblock reorients the upper stage of the gatehouse, in this case, it would appear, to convey a better sense of the enclosed quadrangular space behind. He also regularizes the street front, making it appear symmetrical when the gatehouse here was off-centre. The regular row of windows on the upper floor of the opposite range indicates the library. Bereblock shows the large hall window on the street front, immediately to the left of the tower and he exaggerates the extent of the projection of the chapel from the rear of the site, in order to represent both its large windows. It is known from documentary records that the walls of this college were not of squared stone but of rougher stone, covered with render or rough cast. Bereblock does not differentiate this in his representation. The range to the street was heightened in 1737 and the walls were faced with squared stone in 1804.

Thomas Fowler, *The History of Corpus Christi College* (Oxford, 1893).

FOL. 7ᵛ – MERTON COLLEGE

The drawing of Merton College is dominated by the enormous chapel, whose size forms one of the themes of the accompanying verse. The main body of the chapel dates from the 1290s, but the transepts and bell tower were added in stages over the next 150 years. Bereblock dwells on the dramatic skyline of the belltower, showing the openwork battlements (with quatrefoil frieze below) and tall pinnacles. The bays of the main body of the chapel are carefully plotted, but Bereblock has reduced their number from seven to four. It would be inappropriate to think of this as a 'mistake' and more productive to think of it as a response to the task of making a fine show of a long, wide building site within the proportions of a square-format space. Note the open wicket gate of the chapel door on the south transept, opening on to the street. Merton was unusual in that the college chapel also functioned as a parish church, this door gate serving as the parishioners' entrance.

The chapel appears to dwarf the buildings which surround it: in the background, the hall raised on an undercroft of the 1270s, and in the foreground the gate tower, possibly begun in 1418, with its statuary added in the 1460s, flanked by modest accommodation blocks. Other buildings which made up this complex are not even hinted at. The extensive Warden's Lodgings, situated to the left of the buildings in the drawing, are entirely excluded from the view and no attempt is made to indicate the existence of the small quadrangle that lay behind the chapel. As with the drawing of Magdalen College, Bereblock 'epitomizes' the grandeur within a single view, rather than attempting to include all aspects of the complex.

A. J. Bott and J. R. L. Highfield, 'The Sculpture over the Gatehouse at Merton College, Oxford', *Oxoniensia,* 58 (1993), 233–40; G. H. Martin and J. R. L. Highfield, *A History of Merton College* (Oxford, 1997).

FOL. 6v – ORIEL COLLEGE

As this college was completely rebuilt in the first half of the seventeenth century, Bereblock's view is a valuable record of its earlier form. The viewpoint chosen allows a good view of the newest part of the building, the recently rebuilt hall of c.1534–5, with its large and expensive oriel window lighting the high table end, a further large mullioned and transomed window to the street front and a prominent porch extending into the quadrangle itself. The entrance front, of c.1410–11, appears not to have had a separately expressed gatehouse: this is shown flush with the street front, marked only by the string-course stepping up and over the arch and carvings in the spandrels. The opposite range housed the library on the upper floor, built c.1449. Bereblock shows it very distinctly, as having been lit with large, square-headed cross windows. This may suggest some later remodelling, as this form tends to be reserved for showing the newest fashion of windows, as in the hall porch here or in the windows at Christ Church and the new President's Lodgings at Magdalen. To the right, the chapel of c.1420, shown with exaggeratedly large gable crosses, rises above the rest of this range.

FOL. 10 – QUEENS COLLEGE

In the proposed reconstruction of the manuscript, this would have formed a double-page spread with the image of Oriel.

Queen's College was entirely rebuilt in the eighteenth century and none of the buildings shown here survives. Most of the buildings depicted date from the second half of the fourteenth century: the gate on the street front (now Queen's Lane) and its adjoining chambers, on the left the chapel (1373–80), opposite, a range of chambers, and at the rear of the quadrangle the hall, with three tall windows and projecting porch. The Queen's College site, like that at Merton, was long and wide and, as in that drawing, Bereblock has abbreviated the buildings shown in adapting to the square proportion of the drawing space. The substantial President's Lodging, which lay to the left of the hall, is not shown and a new extension to the chapel, added in 1516, is given only a summary treatment. This antechapel was a large building, larger than the existing chapel, which lay transversely to it, forming a T-shape. This shape is not made evident, although its battlemented parapet, large windows and leaded roof are indicated.

FOL. 10v – UNIVERSITY COLLEGE

University College was entirely rebuilt between 1634 and 1675 and none of the buildings shown here remain. The most emphatic element in Bereblock's view is the large gate tower, possibly built in 1470s but rebuilt or remodelled in the early sixteenth century. It appears to have an unusual proportion – very broad, but only two stages high – and this seems to be confirmed by other representations of it: it is shown thus in Agas's map of Oxford and in the foreground of a drawing of All Souls made in c.1600. The elaborate oriel window in the gate tower originally lit the principal room belonging to the Master. The building shown as extending to the left of the street front was taken over in 1531 to form a separate Master's Lodgings on a much more expansive scale. The interior of the quadrangle shows the hall to the left, the large traceried windows of the chapel (with bell tower) lying opposite the gate, and two square-headed windows on the range adjoining. The view can be compared with a sketch of this corner of the quadrangle made by Anthony Wood c.1668, just before their demolition. It would appear that Bereblock has again abbreviated the view, Wood showing the chapel with three windows rather than two, with buttresses between them.

The word-play on genus and species in the accompanying verse is an 'academic joke' alluding to the categories of formal logic. The statement that the college was founded by King Alfred in 873 asserts the widely held but erroneous belief that the college, and the university itself, was founded in the ninth century.

R. H. Darwall-Smith (ed.), *Account Rolls of University College, Oxford*, 2 vols. (Oxford, 1999); Darwall-Smith, *University College: The first 750 Years* (Oxford, 1999). The drawing of All Souls is reproduced in Colvin and Simmons, *All Souls*, frontispiece.

FOL. 11v – BRASENOSE COLLEGE

The quadrangle at Brasenose was built in 1509–18. The architectural showpiece of the college was the richly panelled gatehouse, and Bereblock's drawing concentrates on this. The college had no separate chapel at this date and its hall was comparatively plain, indicated here only by a fragment of a window immediately to the left of the tower. The street front, with its matching oriel windows at either end, presents a strong symmetrical effect, although Bereblock has enhanced this by regularizing the treatment of the smaller windows. He has also been concerned to indicate the large brick chimney-stacks, which were a distinctive and unusual feature of Brasenose.

The range at the back of the quadrangle contained chambers for the fellows. The description of the upper floor indicates large windows lighting the communal sleeping chamber and smaller windows lighting the individual studies opening off them. This was the standard pattern for fellows' accommodation in the medieval colleges. The two-light windows of the upper floor on the right-hand range indicate the library.

FOL. 12 – LINCOLN COLLEGE

Bereblock's drawing shows the fifteenth-century quadrangle of Lincoln, erected in stages between 1430 and 1479. This is still largely intact, although the street front, to Turl Street, was remodelled in the nineteenth century. The street front has been made to appear symmetrical, as at Corpus and Brasenose, with large, evenly spaced windows. The large traceried windows and prominent buttresses of the hall, on the range opposite the gate, are clearly shown, and the adjoining Rector's Lodging, of 1465–70, indicated by the top of its entrance arch and the large window to its upper chamber (although Loggan shows this as an oriel window). At this date the chapel at Lincoln was not a separate building but a room on the upper floor of the north range of the quadrangle, shown here by the two large two-light windows nearest the hall. A matching pair of windows on the continuation of the range towards the street indicates the original library in upper floor.

FOL. 12^{v} – EXETER COLLEGE

In contrast to the stately sequence of quadrangular buildings which precedes it, Bereblock's drawing of Exeter College reveals its curious topography. At the front of the college site is the gatehouse (Palmer's Tower), with the Rector's Lodging to the east and chambers to the west, built in the 1430s. This gate opened into a narrow lane running between the college and the city wall, just a few yards to the north. (The current westward orientation of the college, as entered from Turl Street, was not definitively established until the seventeenth century.) Parallel to the Rector's Lodging lay the original chapel of the college, consecrated in 1326, which occupied the upper floor of a two-storey building. Bereblock's representation dramatically foreshortens the space between this building and the front range, showing only the heads of the chapel windows. (Note the key-shaped finial on the west gable, derived from the keys of St Peter, Patron of the See of Exeter.) The chimneys serving the chambers below are also indicated.

The lead-roofed wing projecting back at a right angle to the chapel is the old library (1383, extended c.1404). The suggestion of a taller building immediately behind the tower may be intended to represent the old refectory of the college. The stone precinct walls of the college are shown, the battlemented range to the left immediately adjoining the precincts of the Divinity School, but it would appear that the rear part of the site was marked only by a wooden fence.

Of the buildings shown here, all that remain are the gatehouse and a fragment of the lodgings adjoining it to the east, now surrounded by, and partly embedded in, new buildings of the eighteenth, nineteenth and twentieth centuries.

C. W. Boase, *Registrum Collegii Exoniensis* (Oxford, 1894)

FOL. 14 – TRINITY COLLEGE

Formerly Durham College, a Benedictine foundation of c.1290, it was suppressed in 1544, following the dissolution of the monasteries. The buildings were acquired by Sir Thomas Pope for his new foundation, Trinity College, established in 1554–5 during the reign of Mary I (Neale gives 1556, the year the first scholars were admitted). Bereblock's drawing shows the remaining monastic buildings, mostly erected in the first twenty years of the fifteenth century. The quadrangle was set well back from the street, now Broad Street, and from a long a walled lane immediately adjacent to Balliol College. The original chapel and adjoining inner gateway form the front range of the quadrangle. These were replaced by new work in the 1690s. The large windows of the upper floor of the range to the right indicate the library. The shell of this range still survives. The large traceried windows on the opposite range show the original hall of the college, replaced in the early seventeenth century. Bereblock treats these windows frontally, rather than in perspective, producing a curious effect. The range at the rear of the quadrangle, which was rebuilt in the eighteenth century, contained, at the hall end, a parlour below and a warden's chamber above.

The verse accompanying the drawing also lauds Pope's widow, Elizabeth (later Lady Paulet), who is named in the statutes as foundress. After Pope's death she assumed an important role in directing the operations of the college and was herself buried in the college chapel.

C. Hopkins, *Trinity. 450 Years of an Oxford College Community* (Oxford, 2005).

FOL. 14^{v} – BALLIOL COLLEGE

Although the foundation of the college date back to the thirteenth century, the buildings shown here all date from the fifteenth and early sixteenth centuries. Bereblock's raking view emphasizes the gatehouse (c.1495), with its ogee tabernacles and impressive oriel window, and the hall and Master's Lodgings complex in the foreground. Only half of the hall is shown. At right angles to this, between the hall and the street front, is a two-storey building which housed the buttery on the ground floor and a large room above belonging to the Master's accommodation, whose grand window is shown. The curious structure apparently lying at an angle between this and the hall actually stood parallel to the hall and formed a porch, with room over, leading into the hall passage, communicating with the quadrangle and providing access within both to the hall and the buttery. Bereblock has reoriented this to enable a display of the porch. At the rear of the quadrangle lies the relatively new chapel, built in 1522–9 and not fully completed until the mid-1540s, with all three windows, its buttresses, its leaded roof and battlemented skyline. The long library room which formed the continuation of this range, on the upper floor, is, however, suggested by only a single window.

Much of what is shown here was replaced with new buildings in the nineteenth century: only the shell of the hall and library remain, both much restored by Wyatt in the 1790s, who added battlements to both.

The base line on this drawing has been gone over several times, almost scoring through the paper: one of the very rare mistakes in this otherwise carefully prepared manuscript.

In the text Neale confuses the founder, John of Balliol, with his son, John Balliol, King of Scots.

J. Jones, *Balliol College* (Oxford, 1997), esp. 30–34, 47–50, 57—63.

FOL. 15v – ST JOHN'S COLLEGE

Like Trinity College, St John's was also a Marian foundation, established within the property of a dissolved monastic college. St Bernard's College, a house for Cistercian monks studying at Oxford, had been founded by Archbishop Chichele, who was also the founder of All Souls in 1437. Its quadrangle was still incomplete at the time of Sir Thomas White's refoundation in 1555.

Bereblock's drawing shows the battlemented gatehouse with oriel window and arrangement of canopied niches for statuary. As in the representation of many other colleges, the street front has been regularized and the height of the entrance arch itself exaggerated. The two-light windows on each floor of the north and south gable ends of the street front do seem to have been carefully observed and the distinctive string-course above the two upper windows of the north gable, a particular idiosyncrasy of the St John's street front, is still visible today. Of the buildings added after the refoundation in the 1550s, Bereblock shows, opposite the gatehouse, the new east range (incomplete at the time of the dissolution) containing, to the left, the new President's Lodgings, and to the right, a library on the ground floor, with a gallery on the floor above, perhaps intended as a common room for the fellows. Projecting out from the remodelled hall is the new kitchen, with it prominent chimney, and buttery. This was actually an L-shaped arrangement, but here Bereblock represents it at an oblique angle.

H. M. Colvin, 'The Building of St Bernard's College, *Oxoniensia,* 24 (1959), 37–44; W. H. Stevenson and H. E. Salter, *The Early History of St John's College, Oxford* (OHS, n.s., I; Oxford, 1939), 93–110.

FOL. 16v – THE DIVINITY SCHOOL

Built in the fifteenth century to house, on the ground floor, a lecture room for theology with a library room above. Neale's verse celebrates the royal connection with Humfrey of Gloucester, youngest son of Henry IV, who gave his manuscripts to the library, but the financing of the building was drawn from many sources. The spectacular vault of the School Room, completed in the 1480s, is the climax of the verse but no mention is made of the library, which by this time, as a result of the Edwardian reformation, was empty of its manuscripts and its furnishings had been dispersed.

Bereblock 's drawing has been carefully plotted to ensure the representation of a succession of evenly spaced bays: indeed, the proportions of the building as a whole are fairly accurate, but the short ends of the building are shown as straight-headed rather than gabled, as is presumed to have been the case. The drawing also allows us to understand the building prior to the seventeenth-century extensions which enclosed its east and west ends. The east end, where the entrance now is, is not shown, but we are given a clear view of the west end (now enclosed by the Convocation House). The broader turrets, enriched with panelling in the lower stages, housed the stairs which gave access to the library above. These were entered from within a porch formed in the space between the turrets, which appears to have had unglazed traceried openings flanking the central door. The battlemented wall at the base of the drawing represents the precinct wall, not the city wall.

S. Gillam, *The Divinity School and Duke Humfrey's Library in Oxford* (Oxford, 1988); J. N. L. Myres, 'Recent Discoveries in the Bodleian Library', *Archaeologia,* 101 (1967), 151–68.

FOL. 17 – THE PUBLIC SCHOOLS

After the splendours of the Divinity School, the seemingly modest range of the Public Schools is something of an anti-climax, but it was a building of great significance for the university and for the theme of the dialogue. It accommodated the ten lecture rooms, each dedicated to one of the seven liberal arts and the three philosophies (Natural, Metaphysical and Moral). Originally built in 1440 by Oseney Abbey, which rented the rooms out to individual masters as teaching rooms, the Schools passed, after the dissolution, to Christ Church and were thence transferred to the ownership of the university in 1555; by this time they seem to have become badly decayed. Bereblock's drawing records the recent remodelling of the

Schools undertaken in 1557–9 (not, as the verse implies, newly built) under the patronage of Queen Mary. The money for the rebuilding came from a grant of lands given by the Queen to the university in 1556, a donation which trebled the University's annual income. (In comparison with the private wealth of the individual colleges, the University, as a corporate body, was relatively poor.)

Bereblock's view, adapted to the square format of his drawing space, gives a misleadingly modest impression of its length, which was probably near 120 ft, but he is quite precise in recording the tall two- and three-light square-headed windows with hood-moulds, and the new doors, inserted during the reconstruction: their number matches up with those recorded in the surviving building accounts for the reconstruction project. The stippled treatment of the wall surfaces suggests that these were not ashlar, but rough cast or rendered.

The description in Neale's verse, of 'one path which opens the way to all forms of learning' alludes to the creation of the enclosed precinct in front of the Schools, clearly shown in the drawing, and entered under the newly-built battlemented archways at either end. These closed off the northern end of the street in front, which the university had acquired from the city in 1558. This spatial reconfiguration marks the beginning of a process of gradual colonization of this part of the city by university-owned buildings, a process that accelerated in the following century. The old Schools were demolished to make way for the new Schools Quadrangle and extension to the Bodleian Library, begun in 1613.

Oxford University Archives N. W. 3. 6; I. G. Philip, 'Queen Mary Tudor's Benefaction to the University', *Bodleian Library Record,* 5 (1954), 27–36; W. Pantin , 'The Halls and Schools of Medieval Oxford: an Attempt at Reconstruction', in A. B. Emden (ed.), *Oxford Studies Presented to Daniel Callus* (Oxford, 1964), 31–100.

NOTES

1. 'The Receaving of the Quenes Majestie into Oxford, 1566', Corpus Christi College, Oxford, CCC MS. 257, fols. 104–14, transcribed in Bodleian Library, Oxford, Bodl. MS. Twyne 17, 157–67. This eyewitness account of the events of the Royal Visit was composed by Miles Windsor, fellow of Corpus Christi College. See John R. Elliot Jr., 'Queen Elizabeth at Oxford: New Light on the Royal Plays of 1566', *English Literary Renaissance,* 18 (1988), 218–29.

2. The presentation to the Queen is recorded in CCC MS. 257, fol. 108, though Windsor appears to have been unaware that the book contained pictures. It is also recorded in two other contemporary narratives, both in Latin: (i) Nicholas Robinson, Bishop of Bangor, 'Of the Actes done at Oxford when the Queen's Majesty was there' (Folger Shakespeare Library, MS. V.a. 176, later copied in British Library, BL Harl. MS. 7033); (ii) 'Commentarii sive Ephemerae Actiones rerum illustrium Oxonii gestarum in Adventu Serenissimae Principis Elizabethae' (now Bodl. MS. Rawlinson D. 1071). This anonymous account was attributed to John Bereblock by Thomas Hearne, who published it as an appendix to his *Historia Vitae et Regni Ricardi II* (1729). Both were reproduced in John Nichols, *The Progresses, and Public Processions, of Queen Elizabeth* (London, 1788) and again in C. Plummer (ed.), *Elizabethan Oxford: Reprints of Rare Tracts* (Oxford, 1887), 169–92 & 111–50. The accounts of the presentation are on pp. 140 and 183. New critical editions of these texts, with translations from the Latin, will be published in Jayne Archer, Elizabeth Clarke, *et al.* (eds.), *Court and Culture in the Reign of Queen Elizabeth I: A New Critical Edition of John Nichols' 'Progresses of Queen Elizabeth I',* 4 vols. (Oxford, 2007). Page references hereafter will refer to the Plummer edition.

3. Robert Dudley (1532?–88), created Earl of Leicester in September 1564 and appointed Chancellor of the University of Oxford in December of the same year, holding the office until his death. For an account of his life see *Dictionary of National Biography* (Oxford, 2004), hereafter *DNB.*

4. Thomas Neale (1519–90?), Fellow of New College, Oxford, from 1540 (BA 1542, MA 1546, BD 1556). In France in 1556 and possibly some years before. Chaplain to Edmund Bonner, Bishop of London, during Queen Mary's reign he returned to Oxford, possibly in 1558, and was appointed to the Regius Professorship of

NOTES TO PAGE 10

Hebrew in 1559. He resigned the Professorship in 1569 and retired to the village of Cassington, near Oxford. John Bereblock (c.1532, death date unknown) was admitted to St John's College, Oxford, 1559/60, by the founder, Sir Thomas White (BA 1562, MA 1566) and migrated to Exeter College in June 1566, having been appointed Fellow and Dean of the college by Sir William Petre in April of that year. Served as Proctor (with Thomas Bodley), 1569. Granted permission by Petre in 1570 to study abroad for four years, he received BCL from an unknown foreign university in 1572 but appears not to have returned to Oxford. In 1575 he, or a man of the same name, is recorded in Bologna, seeking ordination to the Roman Catholic priesthood, and was still there in 1578. See Andrew Hegarty, The *Biographical Register of St John's College, Oxford: From the Foundation to 1660* (Oxford, forthcoming). I am indebted to Dr Hegarty for his generosity in allowing me to consult his text prior to publication. See also *DNB*, 'Thomas Neale' and 'John Bereblock'.

5. 'istoque illius dono magnopere commovetur, nec antea unquam visa est ullum munus majus meliusve accepisse': from the 'Bereblock' account, Plummer, *Elizabethan Oxford*, 140. This account places the presentation on the Thursday of the Queen's visit; Windsor and Robinson place it on the Tuesday. Neale's gift was, as is stated in the peroration, a private or individual gift, not the formal gift of the university, which, according to Windsor, took the more conventional form of 'six pairs of very fine gloves'.

6. The gift is not recorded in the Bodleian Library Benefactors Register. One possible candidate for the donor could be John More (b. 1589), fourth son of Sir Robert More of Loseley in Surrey, a student at Gloucester Hall in Oxford, 1605–8 (J. Foster, *Alumni Oxonienses, 1500–1714*, 4 vols. (Oxford, 1891–2), vol. 3, 1023). His father and grandfather both had close connections with the court. John's father, Sir Robert, himself an important donor to the Bodleian in 1604, had served Leicester from 1579, and was later in the household of Henry, Prince of Wales. His grandfather, Sir William, had entertained the Queen at Loseley on several occasions (*DNB*, 'Sir George More'; 'Sir William More'). It could be conjectured that the manuscript came into the family as a gift from Leicester or from the Queen herself, or even from Prince Henry.

NOTES TO PAGES 10–11

7. The compilers of the *Bodleian Library Summary Catalogue* (Oxford, 1922), item 3056, were circumspect about the status of the manuscript, as was Plummer (*Elizabethan Oxford,* xvii & n.1.)

8. For discussion of the problems of identifying presentation copies, and of instances of other manuscripts intended for the Queen ending up in other hands, see Carlo Bajetta, 'The Manuscript Collections of Verse Presented to Elizabeth I: A preliminary investigation', *Ben Jonson Journal* 8 (2001), 147–205. See also E. S. Leedham-Green, *Verses presented to Queen Elizabeth I by the University of Cambridge, August 1564: Cambridge University Library MS. Add. 8915* (Cambridge, 1993). This Cambridge book of poems appears to have remained in the possession of Sir William Cecil who, as Chancellor of Cambridge University, had ordered its making.

9. This was noted by David Rogers in *The Bodleian Library and Its Treasures 1320–1700* (Henley-on-Thames, Oxon, 1991), 9. See also *Queen Elizabeth's Oxford: The Bodleian Library Calendar for 1983* (Oxford, 1982). The Neale manuscript in the British Library (BL MS. Royal 2 D. xxi) contains his Latin translations from the Hebrew of Rabbi David Kimhi's commentaries on the minor prophets, together with a dedicatory preface to the Queen. Neale had previously published *Commentarii Rabbi Dauidis Kimhi in Haggæum, Zachariam & Malachiam Prophetas* (Paris, 1557).

10. Rogers, *The Bodleian Library,* 9.

11. The development of topography in sixteenth-century England is discussed in Catherine Delano-Smith and R. J. P. Kain, *English Maps: A History* (London, 1999), especially chapter 3, 'Mapping Country and County' and chapter 6, 'Mapping Towns'.

12. 'Romani palatii amplitudinem ... diceres imitare', as recorded in the 'Bereblock' account, Plummer, *Elizabethan Oxford,* 124.

NOTES TO PAGES 11–12

13. For accounts of the Cambridge visit, see Nichols, *Progresses* (1788, 1823) and Archer & Clarke et al. (eds.), *Court and Culture.* A delegation from Oxford had been present throughout the 1564 Cambridge visit, as indeed had Dudley, not yet Earl of Leicester, but at that time High Steward of Cambridge.

14. Elizabeth's public persona as the learned queen was celebrated in Abraham Hartwell's long verse account of the Royal Visit to Cambridge, *Regina Literata* (London, 1565, STC 12897). On this see J. W. Binns, 'Abraham Hartwell, Herald of the New Queen's Reign: *The Regina Literata* (London, 1565)', in Gilbert Tournoy and Dirk Sacré (eds.), *Ut Granum Sinapis: Essays on Neo-Latin Literature in Honour of Jozef Ijsewijn* (Leuven, 1997), 292–304. For an analysis of Elizabeth's own manipulation of this persona see Linda Shenk, 'Turning Learned Authority into Royal Supremacy: Elizabeth I's Learned Persona and her University Orations', in Carole Levin *et al.* (eds.), *Elizabeth I: Always her Own Free Woman* (Burlington, VT, 2003), 78–96.

15. See, for example, the orations and verses prepared by members of Magdalen College (BL MS. Royal 12 A xlvii), reprinted in Nichols, *Progresses* (1788) and in Plummer, *Elizabethan Oxford,* 207–35. For discussion of university poetry of the period see J. W. Binns, *Intellectual Culture in Elizabethan and Jacobean England: The Latin Writings of the Age* (Leeds, 1990), especially chapter 3.

16. Alistair Fowler, 'The Emblem as a Literary Genre', in Michael Bath and Daniel S. Russell (eds.), *Deviceful Settings: The English Renaissance Emblem and Its Contexts* (New York, 1999), 1–31, at p. 12.

17. A very small number of dialogue verses and eclogues is included in volumes of gratulatory poems presented to the Queen by Eton College in 1563 (Nichols, *Progresses,* 1788, B-H 5, 1–51) and by Cambridge University in 1564 (Leedham-Green, *Verses presented to Queen Elizabeth*). See also Archer, Clarke et *al., Court & Culture* (2007). Although the Queen appears as interlocutor in some of these, her companions are generalized figures or personifications. An interesting near-contemporary example of innovative use of the dialogue form is found in Gerard Legh's account of the Christmas Revels at the Inner Temple, London 1561–2,

NOTES TO PAGES 12–14

presided over by Dudley (*Accedens of Armory* (London, 1562), STC 15388). This is told through the conceit of an imaginary traveller's tale, using nested dialogue in the manner of More's *Utopia.* I am indebted to Michelle O'Callaghan for bringing this text to my attention.

18. The complex etiquette of real-person or 'documentary' dialogues and the Ciceronian models on which they were based is analysed in Virginia Cox, *The Renaissance Dialogue: Literary Dialogue in its Social and Political Contexts, Castiglione to Galileo* (Cambridge, 1992), especially chapter 4. Cox notes the relative rarity of documentary dialogues in English writing of the period (pp. 22–3).

19. Castiglione's *Cortegiano* was first published in Venice in 1528. It was clearly known in England from an early date (cf. Thomas Elyot's *The Boke called the Governor,* 1531, STC 7635) and was popularized through Sir Thomas Hoby's English translation, *The Courtyer of Count Baldassar Castilio* (London, 1561).

20. Similar word-play is found in two poems addressed to Robert Dudley on his creation as Earl of Leicester; by Walter Haddon (Nichols, *Progresses,* 1788, B-H, 48) and by Charles Utenhove in Johan Radermacher's Album Amicorum (Centrale Bibliotheek, University of Ghent, MS. 2464, fol. 95. The Haddon poem also appears on 95^{v}.)

21. The current physical structure of the manuscript shows it to have been so altered that it is no longer possible to establish with certainty its original order, but it is significant that the disruption is most evident in fols. 5–9, where the obviously misplaced verses appear. These folios are no longer conjoint, and have all been attached to fol. 5. A close copy of Neale's dialogue, but without the prefatory material or the Hebrew text, is transcribed in Bodl. MS. Twyne 21, 779–92. The hand and date are uncertain, but it may have come to Twyne through Miles Windsor who gave his papers to Twyne in the early seventeenth century. Windsor had earlier published another version of the verses on the colleges and schools in his *Academiarum Quae Aliquando Fuere Et Hodie Sunt in Europa, Catalogus & Enumeratio Breuis* (London, 1590), 42–8 and, from a note in an earlier draft of his account of the Royal Visit (CCC MS. 257, fols. 115–23, at 119^{v}), it would ap-

NOTES TO PAGES 14–15

pear that he had originally intended to include these in the final version of that account. Windsor's rough draft is analysed, and selections from it reproduced, in Elliot 'New Light' and in Elliot *et al.* (eds.), *Records of Early English Drama: Oxford,* 2 vols. (Toronto, Oxford, 2004), vol. 1, 126–35; vol. 2, 696–7.

22. The relative wealth of the colleges in 1566 can be partly deduced from a table of incomes drawn up in 1592, in order to assess the proportionate contribution each college should make to the costs of the Queen's visit to Oxford in that year. Christ Church, with a foundation of over a hundred members, headed the list with a huge annual income of £2,000, twenty times that of Balliol and University College at the bottom (foundations of twenty and ten members respectively). The first six colleges in Neale and Bereblock's (reconstructed) itinerary are, indeed, those that head the 1592 list. See G. E. Aylmer, 'The Economics and Finances of the Colleges and University c.1530–1640', in J. McConica (ed.), *The Collegiate University (The History of the University of Oxford,* vol. 3 (Oxford, 1986), 523–4. The list is printed in J. M. Fletcher (ed.), *Registrum Annalium Collegii Mertonensis, 1567–1603* (Oxford, 1976), 287.

23. According to Anthony Wood, Neale built himself two rooms here. (*Athenae Oxonienses,* vol. 1, 576).

24. For Petre's career see F. G. Emmison, *Tudor Secretary: Sir William Petre at Court and Home* (London, 1961).

25. 'Quae, quales, quantosque tibi promittat alumnos/ Ex uno disci caetera turba potest. / Is Bereblokus erit, cujus dexterrima dextra/ has formas mira dexteritate dedit' (fol. 13^{v}).

26. Bereblock had been a Fellow of both St John's and Exeter, and Neale had been financially supported by Sir Thomas White. St John's was founded in 1555, during Mary's reign and Bereblock's and Neale's Oxford connections suggest strong Catholic associations. Petre and White had pronounced Catholic sympathies and St John's and Exeter both had reputations as Catholic strongholds. Neale had been a chaplain to Bishop Bonner during Mary's reign, and was the nephew of

NOTES TO PAGES 16–18

the Catholic Alexander Belsyre, first President of St John's College. See note 4 above.

27. Nichols, *Progresses* (1823), vol. 1, 178. Copies of the speeches circulated in manuscript and a permanent record of the proceedings was available in Abraham Hartwell's *Regina Literata.*

28. 'Stokys' Book', Cambridge University Library, University Archives: Misc.Collect.4, fol. 74^{v}, cited in Leedham-Green, *Verses Presented to Queen Elizabeth,* i.

29. Leicester, and many other members of the Royal party, including the Spanish Ambassador, did make visits to the Schools and to many of the colleges where they were received with entertainments and orations. See the accounts by Windsor, 'Bereblock' and Robinson.

30. For the political agenda of the visits see Binns, 'Abraham Hartwell', 295, and Mary Hill Cole, *The Portable Queen: Elizabeth I and the Politics of Ceremony* (Amherst, MA, 1999), 138–40. Eleanor Rosenberg, in *Leicester, Patron of Letters* (New York, 1955), 124, analysed the dedicatory preface to Leicester in the great Latin dictionary published by Thomas Cooper of Magdalen, the *Thesaurus Linguae Romanae et Britannicae* (1565), STC 5686, as 'a gloss on the queen's speech at Cambridge', emphasizing Oxford's 'readiness to share in the royal promises as well as the royal reforms'. Leicester was hailed in the preface as a chief architect of the new policy and patron of learning.

31. E.g. Plummer, *Elizabethan Oxford,* xvi: 'I fear the modern reader will not derive very much pleasure from either Neale's verses or Bereblock's drawings'.

32. See W. H. Stevenson and H. E. Salter, *The Early History of St John's College, Oxford* (Oxford, 1939), 142–3. The authors erroneously describe the Trinity image as a picture of Queen Elizabeth and John the Baptist.

33. The regularizing of the windows is deduced from comparison with the Loggan engravings of colleges, published in 1675.

NOTES TO PAGES 22–23

34. New College, Oxford MS. C. 288, on deposit in Bodleian Library. The manuscript of c.1464 is a commemoration of the acts of William of Wykeham, founder of New College, made for presentation to Thomas Bekynton, Bishop of Bath and Wells, by Thomas Chaundler, Warden of New College. The identity of the draughtsman is unknown. K. C. Scott, *Later Gothic Manuscripts, 1390–1490*, 2 vols. (*A Survey of Manuscripts Illuminated in the British Isles*, vol. 6, London, 1996, vol. 1, 424–5 [ills.]; vol. 2, 310–13 [text]. Scott remarks that the specificity of the architectural descriptions is unusual in English manuscripts of this period. The manuscript was acquired by New College sometime between 1598 and 1624.

35. As, for example, in von Breydenbach's *Peregrinatio in Terram Sanctam* (Mainz, 1486) or in the illustrations of towns included in Sebastian Munster's *Cosmographiae Universalis* (Basel, 1550) or Antoine du Pinet's *Plantes, Pourtraits et descriptions de plusieurs villes, forteresses, tant de l'Europe Asie, Afrique que des Indes et Terres Neuves* (Lyons, 1564). For detailed analyses of the meanings and functions of these city views see Jurgen Schultz, 'Jacopo de Barbari's View of Venice: Map-making, city views and moralized geography before the year 1500', *Art Bulletin* 60 (1978), 425–74; Lucia Nuti, 'The Perspective Plan in the Sixteenth Century: The Invention of a Representational Language', *Art Bulletin* 76/1 (1994), 106–128; Thomas Frangenberg, 'Chorographies of Florence: The Use of City Views and City Plans in the 16th Century', *Imago Mundi,* 47 (1995), 41–64.

36. See Peter Barber, 'England I: Pageantry, Defence and Government: Maps at Court to 1550' and 'England II: Monarchs, Ministers and Maps', in David Buisseret (ed.), Monarch*s, Ministers and Maps: The Emergence of Cartography as a Tool of Government in Early Modern Europe* (Chicago, 1992), 26–56; 57–98; Delano-Smith and Kain, *English Maps,* 179–200; Stan Mendyk, 'Early British Chorography', *Sixteenth Century Journal,* 17/4 (1986), 459–81.

37. William Cuningham, *The Cosmographical Glasse: Conteinyng the Pleasant Principles of Cosmographie, Geographie, Hydrographie, or Nauigation* (London, 1559) STC 6119. Cuningham dedicated the work to Lord Robert Dudley, as he then was. The book and its illustrations are discussed in C.L. Oastler, *John Day, Elizabethan Printer* (Oxford Bibliographical Society, Occasional Publications 10;

NOTES TO PAGES 23–26

Oxford, 1975) and in S. K. Heninger Jnr., *The Cosmographical Glass, Renaissance Diagrams of the Universe* (San Marino, CA, 1977). The mapping of London is discussed in Ann Saunders and John Schofield, *Tudor London: A Map and a View* (London, 2001).

38. See note 63 below, where I identify a possible copy made by Bereblock of an image from Cuningham's book.

39. For Leicester's mathematical interests see *DNB* and Eleanor Rosenberg, *Leicester, Patron of Letters* (1955), 30–32. Whether Leicester may actually have had a hand in encouraging the making of the Topographical Delineation, and its associated map, cannot be known. William Cecil's interests in, and practical use of, maps and mapping is well known. See Barber, 'England II'.

40. For evidence of scholarly interest in maps and mapping at this date see Catherine Delano-Smith, 'Map Ownership in 16th Century Cambridge: The Evidence of Probate Inventories', *Imago Mundi,* 47 (1995), 67–93.

41. See Nuti, 'Perspective Plan', and Nuti, 'Mapping Places: Chorography and Vision in the Renaissance', in Denis Cosgrove (ed.), *Mappings* (London 1999), 90–108.

42. A detailed analysis of these epistemological debates is provided in Nuti, 'Perspective Plan'.

43. Ibid., 107.

44. It is significant that the language in the 'Bereblock' account of the description of Bereblock's drawings of each of the buildings, '*genuinis picturis naturalem eorum situm ac formam indicantibus*' (Plummer, *Elizabethan Oxford,* 140) echoes the vocabulary of 'truth claims' made in the titles of many of the city views of the period, with phrases such as 'true portrait' or 'true picture'. These titles are discussed in Nuti, 'Perspective Plan', 107–9.

NOTES TO PAGE 27

45. CCC MS. 257, fol. 109.

46. Plummer, *Elizabethan Oxford,* 185. Curiously, the 'Bereblock' narrative seems to make no mention of it.

47. The Vice Chancellor's accounts for 1577–8 record a payment of £20 to Agas for the 'description of Oxford'. I am indebted to David Sturdy for discussion of the Agas Map. The original drawing is lost and the only surviving impression of the printed Agas Map is held by the Bodleian Library. It was re-engraved and printed in 1728 by Robert Whittlesey as *Oxonia Antiqua Instaurata,* with a border of inaccurate and embellished versions of the Bereblock drawings, there attributed to Neale.

48. St John's College Register, vol. 2, 604, entry for 28 August 1616. The link between the map of Oxford and the picture at St John's was first made by Anthony Wood in the late seventeenth century (*Athenae Oxonienses,* ed P. Bliss, London, 1813-20, vol. 1, 577–8), although, having read Twyne's transcript of Miles Windsor's account (Bodl. MS. Twyne 17, 157–67), he believed it to have been the work of Thomas Neale. The picture had been given to the college by one William Nutbrowne, a commoner there in 1580–1 (W. C. Costin, *The History of St John's College, Oxford, 1598–1860* (Oxford, 1958), 7), probably in 1600 when his own two sons came up to the college. William was probably the son of William Nutbrowne Senior of Stanway Hall, near Colchester, in whose will he and his two sons are mentioned (3 November 1588, PRO/PROB/11/73). I have been unable to draw any conclusive connections between Neale, Bereblock and the Nutbrownes that would account for the migration of the 'Grate Picture' from Oxford to Essex, though they would certainly have known the Petre family based at Ingatestone. An alternative hypothesis, that the St John's picture was in some way associated with the Agas Map of 1578, should also be considered. (Agas practised as an estate surveyor in Essex and Suffolk; see *DNB,* 'Ralph Agas'). He could have acquired or been given the 1566 map of Oxford at the time he was making his survey. It is certainly remarkable that some of Bereblock's idiosyncracies also appear in the Agas Map (e.g. the canted tower of Christ Church; the extreme foreshortening of the chapel range at Exeter; the four-bayed treatment of Merton Chapel). Or perhaps the St John's picture could have been a copy of Agas's original survey.

NOTES TO PAGES 27–29

49. SJCA College Register, vol. 2, 604.

50. 'Optimus arte delineandi, ut multae extant descriptiones, praecipue civitatis Roffensis per se delineata', SJCA FN. V.A.12, 'Account of the Fellows of St John's. A', 3. The description appears in an annotation to Bereblock's entry in the list of fellows inserted by William Laud, President of the college 1611–21, and the negotiator of the deal with Sir Thomas Lake for the 'grate picture'. I am most grateful to Michael Riordan, the college archivist, for his generous assistance with interpreting the St John's documents.

51. This was the view taken by Falconer Madan in his preface to a nineteenth-century facsimile of the manuscript, *Collegiorum Scholarumque Publicarum Academiae Oxoniensis, Topographica Delineatio* (Oxford, privately published by J. Guggenheim, 1882), viii.

52. The verses associated with St John's and Exeter colleges have been much abbreviated from the long versions given in the manuscript, and in each case contain additional text not found there.

53. Frangenberg, 'Chorographies of Florence', 44; Shultz, 'Barbari's View', 467–72. In considering the continuities of purpose between chorography, history and encomium in the period it can be revealing to draw a comparison between the lists of physical, architectural and historical features of places, described in contemporary geographical texts as forming the subject matter of chorography, with the formulas codified in manuals of rhetoric for encomia of cities. Richard Rainolde, for example (*The Foundacions of Rhetorike* [London, 1563], STC 20604), in his discussion of 'The parte of Rhetoricke, called praise', lists the topics to be covered in the praise of cities as 'the goodlie situacion of it', 'the wealthe and aboundance, the noble and famous gouvernours, which have governed the same. The first authors and builders of the same, the politike lawes, and goodlie statutes therein maintained: the felicitie of the people, their manners ... the buildyng and ornatures of the same, with Castles, Towers, Havens, Floodes, Temples'. He also included in this category of city praise the 'thwoo famous Universities of this lande, from the whiche, no small nomber of greate learned men and famous, have in the common wealthe sprong, with all other thynges to it' (fol. 38).

NOTES TO PAGES 29–30

54. A further demonstration of the close association between map-making and historical writing is found in the making of the first printed map of Cambridge, commissioned from Richard Lyne by Archbishop Matthew Parker and published in the 1574 edition of John Caius's *Historiae Cantebrigiensis Academiae* (London, STC 4349), together with a new edition of Caius' *De Antiquitate Cantebrigiensis* (STC 4345). This latter text arose out of an ongoing dispute between Oxford and Cambridge over which was the more ancient foundation, a dispute fanned into life by assertions made before the Queen by each party during their respective Royal Visits. Lyne's bird's-eye view bears a long prose inscription ascribing the foundation of Cambridge to Cantaber, a legendary pre-Christian Spanish king. See Henry R. Plomer, 'The 1574 Edition of Dr. John Caius's *De Antiquitate Cantebrigiensis Academiae Libri Duo*', *Library,* VII (1926), 253—68; James Parker, *The Early History of Oxford 727–1100* (OHS, vol. 3, Oxford, 1885), 20–39.

55. See, for example, the portrait of the founder, Richard Fox, at Corpus Christi College, Oxford (Joannes Corvus, c.1530–2?) or the portrait of Robert Dudley on the verso of the title page to William Fulke and Ralph Lever, *The Philosopher's Game* (London, 1563, STC 15542). The classical model for the fashion was Varro's *Imagines,* as described in Cicero and Pliny. Other examples of albums of portraits of famous men are Paulo Giovio, *Elogia viroroum literis illustrium...* (Basle, 1575 and later edns.); Reusner, *Icones sive Imagines virorum literis illustrium* (Strasbourg, 1587); Boissard, *Icones virorum illustrium* (Frankfurt, 1597–9).

56. For a thorough discussion of the prevalence of emblematic habits of thinking in early modern English culture and the rhetorical practices which shaped this, see Michael Bath, *Speaking Pictures: English Emblem Books and Renaissance Culture* (London, 1994), especially chapter 2.

57. The five Regius Professorships, in Theology, Divinity, Hebrew, Greek, and Civil Law were definitively established in 1546. The professors were appointed directly by the crown. See G. D. Duncan, 'Public Lectures and Professorial Chairs' in McConica (ed.), *The Collegiate University,* 335–61.

58. The scriptural allusion, to Psalm 1:3 is also intended. Another example of emblematic strategies appears in Laurence Humphrey's poem in the Magdalen

NOTES TO PAGE 32

volume presented to the Queen (BL Royal MS. 12 A xlvii). This is accompanied by a drawing of the Queen's arms and heraldic badges whose symbolism, as revelatory of the Queen's own virtues, is explicated in the verse.

59. As described in the 'Bereblock' account, Plummer, *Elizabethan Oxford*, 139–40.

60. The manuscript is now in the British Library: see *The Emblems of Thomas Palmer, Sloane MS. 3794, edited with an introduction and notes by John Manning* (New York, 1988), ii, xxxiii. Dudley's association with the early adoption of emblems and imprese at the Elizabethan court is discussed in Alan R. Young, 'The English Tournament Imprese' in P. M. Daly (ed.), *The English Emblem and the Continental Tradition* (New York, 1988), 61–81. The first printed emblem book composed by an English author was Geffrey Whitney's *A Choice of Emblems* (Leiden, 1586), also dedicated to Leicester.

61. Although Manning notes that Bereblock 'did some drawings of Oxford Colleges in 1566', he would appear to have believed these to be no longer extant. John Bettes the Elder, the portrait painter and engraver, is also suggested as an alternative, but less favoured, identification for 'IB' (*Emblems of Thomas Palmer*, xxxiii.)

62. The drawing of Troy in emblem 95, for example, reveals the same delight in crocketed pinnacles evident in Bereblock's college drawings and even employs the identical shorthand notation for iron-bound gates seen in his picture of Magdalen College. His characteristic 'fishscale' roof pattern is also seen in emblem 98 (BL MS. Sloane 3794, fols. 55, 56^{v}). I am currently preparing a more detailed study of the Bereblock/Palmer collaboration for publication as a separate essay.

63. Manning identified the sources for the paste-ins as Barthelemy Aneau, *Picta Poesis* (Lyons, 1552); Claude Paradin, *Heroica Symbola* (Antwerp, 1562); Petrus Costalius, *Pegma* (Lyons, 1555) and two editions of Alciato: the 1542 Paris edition (Wolfgang Hunger's German edition) and the Lyons, 1556 edition (with Stockhamer's commentary). He also noted that two of the drawings, including one with the IB monogram, were copied from Valeriano's *Hieroglyphica* (Basle,

NOTES TO PAGE 32

1556). I can also identify the source for the drawing of Atlas in emblem 5 ('Bear and Forbear' 'A poosee for a prince', fol. 25^{v}), as the woodcut on fol. 50 of William Cuningham's *Cosmographical Glasse.* The derivation of the *pictura* for an emblem so directly addressed to Dudley's personal qualities from another book dedicated to him suggests a deliberate compliment.

64. E.g. Plummer, *Elizabethan Oxford,* xvii; Rogers, *Bodleian Library,* 19.